Palazzi and Villas of Rome

i piccoli
di arsenale

Caroline Vincenti Montanaro
Andrea Fasolo

Palazzi

and Villas

of Rome

arsenale editrice

Caroline Vincenti Montanaro [CVM]
Andrea Fasolo [AF]
PALAZZI AND VILLAS OF ROME

fotography
Roberto Schezen

layout
Stefano Grandi

print
EBS Editoriale Bortolazzi-Stei
Verona

first edition
March 1999

Arsenale Editrice srl
San Polo 1789
I – 30125 Venice
Italy

Arsenale Editrice © 1999

Photo credits

Michele Crosera, Venice, pp. 11, 12, 14-
17, 23, 24-27, 33, 34-35, 41, 43, 45, 61,
63, 65, 66-67, 73, 80-81, 83, 97, 99,
105, 107, 123, 125, 127, 133, 153, 155,
157, 165,176-177, 179, 181, 183, 185,
187

Araldo De Luca, Rome, p. 135

ISBN 88-7743-202-0

Contents

Introduction

Rome has always been an extraordinarily important centre in terms of architectural experimentation, and it has offered emblematic definitions for the typology of both the *palazzo* and the villa forms. To make the reader's work that little bit easier, this volume lists the buildings in alphabetical order. Each detailed description is accompanied by a wealth of illustrations for each of the 60 Roman buildings covered, which span from the 15th to the 19th centuries.

If, in the 15th century, architects of the calibre of Francesco del Borgo (Palazzo Venezia) and Baccio Pontelli (Palazzo della Cancelleria), maintain the dichotomy between the external aspects (which are typologically still mediaeval) and the internal aspects (where the monumental halls assume classical forms), then in the 19th century both Sangallo and Michelangelo attempt to give life to Bramante's idea that modern form has to revive the grandiose and monumental forms of antiquity (see, for example, Palazzo Farnese).

Therefore, the Renaissance is the apex of culture and also of new architectural developments. Commissioners are prevalently members of the upper clerical echelons, while those who are called upon to realise these projects are architects and artists such as Bramante, Raffaello, Antonio da Sangallo the Younger, Francesco Salviati, Baldassarre Peruzzi, Jacopo Sansovino, Michelangelo and Giulio Romano. Their task was to build and decorate an amazing number of palazzi, and to transform what had once been simple pavilions set in urban or suburban plots of land into veritable villas, thus bringing together two typologies that had formerly seemed so distinct and incompatible.

The transition that took place between the 16th and 17th centuries is emblematically represented by Palazzo Barberini, where Carlo Maderno introduces spatial, typological and decorative innovations that would later be taken to their extreme perfection by Bernini, Borromini and Pietro da Cortona.

The period from the 17th to the late 18th centuries, with examples such as Palazzo Falconieri, Palazzo Montecitorio, Villa Pamphili, Villa Borghese and Palazzo della Consulta, brings to life a creative vivacity that "in the Eternal City, home of all Classicism by way of the remains of past splendour, [attempted to] overturn from within the very foundations of the myth of classicism" (P Portoghesi, *Roma Barocca*, 1976).

What must have seemed to the eyes of those experiencing the early Renaissance simply a "seascape of run-down buildings" interspersed with a series of classical Roman remains, mediaeval towers and new buildings currently under construction now seems to us to be a continuous urban texture born of the 18th and 19th centuries.

Obviously, as vast a theme as ours cannot possibly be exhaustively covered in such a limited number of pages; however, we hope that the detailed descriptions and bibliography will tempt the reader to set out on his or her own discoveries and analysis of the palazzi that Rome ultimately owes its eternal splendour to.

1 – Palazzo Alberini (16th century)
via del Banco di Santo Spirito, 12

By the end of the 13th century, when the Alberini family owned houses in the Ponte region, Cecchus Lelli Donati de Ylperinis attempted to reclaim the property that had been confiscated from another family member, Natolo Buci Natoli. Natoli had been beheaded in 1399 for having conspired against the Pope. We know very little about how the Alberini family made use of their property up to this time, though by 1512, Via dei Banchi had been widened. Via dei Banchi was of great commercial interest and it was where the major banks had their offices. This alone gave the heir the opportunity to use the property in the most profitable manner. The houses owned by Giulio Alberini, inherited by his father a few years earlier, were pulled down in order to make room for a *palazzo*, where the ground floor was assigned to the head offices of the major banks. On the upper floors apartments were built for some of the banking families, like the Rucellai and Strozzi families. Raffaello Sanzio was put in charge of building the *palazzo*. According to Frommel, Raffaello worked on a construction in 1518 that had already been started in 1515. The work of Raffaello and of his assistant, Giulio Romano is recognizable above all in the two upper floors. They comprise one solid strip marked by a projecting cornice, which creates a counterbalance to the floor with the shops, which is covered by an original smooth ashlar work. Above the cornice there is the outline of a gallery. The Alberini family died out in 1600 and the *palazzo* was passed on to the Cicciaporci family and then on to the Calderari family. After which it was handed over to the Senni family, who in 1901 passed it on to the Papal College of Portugal. [AF]

2 – Palazzo Aldobrandini Chigi (16th-17th centuries)
Piazza Colonna

In the 17th and 18th centuries Palazzo Chigi was the center of Roman daily life. Great revelry and festive receptions were held there for members of high society, from both artistic and political worlds. During carnival period, the people would wait for food and delicacies that had been in abundance in the sumptuous banquets to be thrown from the balconies. The Aldobrandini family started the construction of the building in 1578, when they bought a house on the main street. They later bought some of the confining area, and they had it enlarged by Giacomo Della Porta and Carlo Maderno. In 1621, Palazzo Chigi was given to Cardinal Giovanni Deti, on the condition that he "make great and varied valuable improvements" to it, and in 1630, the year of the Cardinal's death, Palazzo Chigi once more returned to the Aldobrandini family. In 1659, Dominico Chigi, brother to Pope Alessandro VII, bought the building, which was later enlarged by the architect Felice Della Greca.

It took over a century to complete the grand *palazzo*. Paintings and decorations adorned the architectural structure. The façade with thirteen windows overlooking the main street and towards the centre is considered the main façade. The façade that faces the square, with twelve windows, was given more visibility only after the shacks that stood between the façade and the column had been pulled down. During the 1700s the corner balcony was covered by an elegant *mignano*.

In 1917 Luigi Ludovico Chigi Della Rovere Albani sold the *palazzo* to the Italian State, where it was used for the Colonial Office, then the Foreign Ministry and finally for the Presidency of the Cabinet. [AF]

3 – Palazzo Altemps (16th-17th centuries)
Piazza Sant'Apollinare, 8

Cardinal Girolamo Riario built Palazzo Altemps in 1480. Around 1520 it was bought from the Cardinal by Volterra Francesco Soderini who expanded the building by commissioning Antonio da Sangallo il Vecchio to work on the construction of the main courtyard. In 1568 the Altemps

Pedro Berruguete, fresco in the room of the Piattaia (1480-1481)

family, originally German and very influential in the ecclesiastical courts, bought the building. The following year, Giulio da Bologna, was commissioned to follow through with the new work which was finished, after the intervention of numerous well-known artists, in 1648. The construction of the building took almost two centuries. The massive proportions of the building, due to its asymmetrical irregularity, does not permit an overall view at the same time, and resembles the installation of a 14th century fort. The views scan three levels and the corner that looks towards Piazza Dell'Appollinare is framed by an imposing roof terrace. This is the first recognizable and characteristic element of the work of Palazzo Altemps, by Onorio Longhi. A pilaster strip that ends in a dome with the family coat of arms of the Altemps family which is a climbing ram covers the roof terrace. This in turn is decorated with four small obelisks at the sides. Going through the lobby which has a circular vault, which has four doors, squared by marble frames of the Renaissance era, you enter a portico that is made up of five arches that in turn opens up to the smaller side of the courtyard. At the two extremes you have access to the halls on the ground floor, on one side, and the halls on the first floor by crossing the monumental staircase. The courtyard is composed of four arches, decorated with various sculpted coats of arms, each with three sequences, supported by a series of golden pilaster strips at ground level and at the upper level decoration pertaining to the Ionic order. While the attic, prob-

ably the work of Peruzzi, is characterized by a scanty linearity. The antique sculptures that line the courtyard in a gradual manner, are part of a collection of the Altemps family. Palazzo Altemps was also home to one of the oldest theatres of Rome, where Girolamo Riario first presented his work in the 15th century. In the 1600s Giovanni Angelo Altemps built a twenty-meter long theatre semi-underground, which was most probably built on the occasion of the Roman sojourn in 1770, of the Venetian playwright Carlo Goldoni. It was at this time the theatre changed its name from "Altemps" to "Goldoni". In the 16th century the *palazzo* went through a period of splendor when Cardinal Polignac, then French Minister of Rome, rented it. Polignac was known to have held sumptuous banquets on two memorable occasions. One to celebrate the marriage of the King of France with Maria di Polonia, and the other to commemorate the birth of their first son. On this occasion over three thousand guests participated. The party was held both in Palazzo Altemps and Piazza Novana while wine was serve from the fountain in piazza Sant' Appollinare.

After this period the Altemps family did little to the structure of the *palazzo*, which fell into disrepair until it was bought by the Holy See, which took care of some of the cultural establishments.

In the second half of the 20th century, the Italian Government bought Palazzo Altemps and it is now where the National Museum of Rome has its department of the History of Antique Sculpture collection. [AF]

4 – Palazzo Altieri (17th-18th centuries)

Piazza del Gesù, 49

The original nucleus of today's *palazzo* was built at the request of Cardinal Giovanni Battista Altieri in 1650. The commission went to Giovanni Antonio de' Rossi, an architect who later rose to be one of the leading architects in Rome during the late seventeenth century.

Then came the family's decision to enlarge the *palazzo* and incorporate into it various holdings that they had acquired. One of Emilio's brothers was unexpectedly made a cardinal, and he bequeathed 18.000 scudi toward the restoration of the *palazzo*. For this new work the family again turned to Giovanni Antonio de' Rossi. He planned the enlargement of the building following a plan designed to incorporate the entire city block, creating a single grandiose structure. The portal, surmounted by the family's coat of arms, opened onto an elegant courtyard with a cornice covered by heraldic stars and turtles. The main stairway is sober and elegant, following harmonious proportions and illuminated by large windows. The niches were decorated with antique sculptures from the collection begun by Marc Antonio Altieri. The two monumental courtyards were also joined. Fearing that the pope did not have long to live, the family members grew desperate to complete the ambitious *palazzo* at all costs, ordering that work should continue through the night. In this way a complex and spacious new building came into being, planned under the gaze of its owner, who oversaw the conversion of the home "from cardinal's *palazzo* to the seat of the court of a papal family." As the last male member of the Altieri family, the pope had adopted the Roman nobleman Gasparo Paluzzo degli Albertoni, and it was Gasparo's uncle, Paluzzo Paluzzi degli Albertoni, who directed the construction of this new building. The cardinal's apartment was in the new wing, of course, its walls covered by stuccoes by Ercole Ferrata and precious fabrics. The roomy, sunny areas were in sharp contrast to the old-fashioned, somber rooms of Cardinal Giovanni Battista Altieri, who had expressed the desire for decoration "darkly shaded, suitable for the memory of ancestors," rather than anything that would glorify the power of the new Altieri.

The monumental decorative cycle began halfway into the seventeenth cen-

tury and was carried on for a century over progressively covering the numerous rooms. The main theme was the celebration of Rome, ancient and modern, Christian and pagan. The great hall was ready to be frescoed in 1673, and its ceiling offered ample space for the painter's skilled allegories. Following the deaths of Paluzzo and Clement X, Gasparo Altieri decided to leave Rome for Venice, thus bringing an end to all acquisitions. In 1735, his son, Girolamo, began the work again with the renovation of several of the halls. Felice Giani, as well as some of the most prestigeous artists of Rome, thus worked on the rooms of this 18th century *palazzo* – and each of them demonstrated a deep love of the ancient. [CVM]

5 – Palazzo del Banco di Santo Spirito (16th century)
Via del Banco di Santo Spirito, 31

The *palazzo* was originally the seat of the Papal Mint, as ordered by Guilio II. Bramante and Antonio da Sangallo the Younger both worked on the project. Antonio da Sangallo the Younger worked on the front of the building which is slightly concave.

This work was started under the order of Leo X and completed during the reign of Pope Clement VII. The front of the building is composed of thick ashlar work and a motif of high pilaster Corinthian strips separates the large central arch from the side windows. This is a visible fulcrum of the two axes that come from Sant'Angelo bridge and from the church of San Giovanni dei Fiorentini.

The mint remained at the *palazzo* until 1541. In 1605, Paul V founded the Banco di Santo Spirito, which became the financial support for the Hospital of Santo Spirito, an important organization for religious and social assistance.

On the right of the building there is a plaque that records the artistic work Benvenuto Cellini rendered the Papal Mint. [AF]

6 – Palazzo Barberini (17th century)
Piazza Barberini

The Barberini family, originally from Florence, had resided in Rome since the 15th century. The family became famous when, in 1623, Cardinal Maffeo Barberini became Pope Urban VIII. The *palazzo* emerged at the same place as the villa of Cardinal Rodolfo Pio da Capri and later villa Sforza. Maderno (1556- 1629) started it in 1625, and then Borromini continued the work, which was eventually taken over and finally finished by Bernini, in 1633. Francesco Barberini used bricks and tiles from the Coliseum and the Pantheon to build the *palazzo*, which led to the well-known epigram by Pasquino: "Quod non fecerunt Barbari, fecerunt Barberini". In 1645 a year after the death of Urban VIII, an investigation was started in order to ascertain the public finances of the Barberini administration, which ended with the accusation of embezzlement.

Francesco Borromini, The helicoidal staircase >

The building is composed of a central part by Bernini. The upper windows with a splay perspective, and the back façade are works by Borromini, and they are embedded in the two wings of the *palazzo* which is the work of Maderno. The circular flight of stairs with twin columns by Borromini on the right side of the *palazzo* is of interest, as is the grand staircase on the left. Both staircases lead to symmetrical landings, which take you to the main hall (500 m²) that was magnificently frescoed in 1633 and in 1639 by Pietro da Cortona. This fresco is probably the most brilliant Baroque decoration in a Roman *palazzo*.

In 1949 the *palazzo* was bought by the Italian State, which has assigned one portion of the building to the National Gallery of Antique Art, and another part to the Officers Club. [AF]

Pietro da Cortona, *The Triumph of Divine Providence* (1633-1639) >

7 – Casino Boncompagni Ludovisi
Via Lombardia, 46

Ludovico Ludovisi chose the ancient area of the gardens of Sallust as the site for what he intended to be Rome's most spectacular villa. Alessandro Ludovisi, Ludovico's uncle, was elected pope as Gregory XV (1621–23). He built his home "in only thirty months and surrounded it with pleasing pathways," as a chronicler reported. Cardinal Ludovico extended his property to take in the land and buildings of the Capponi and Del Nero families, eventually extending it over an area of thirty acres. Five lesser buildings were located in the garden, along with fountains and ancient statues.

All that remains today of this extraordinary, boundless villa is one of the lesser buildings, the Casino dell'Aurora. It was probably designed by

Guercino, *Night*, side lunette >

Maderno, and is cruciform, composed of a main central room giving on to four smaller rooms joined on the upper floor by a circular stairway. On top of the building is a lookout tower. Guercino (1591–1666) began working on the decoration in 1621, assisted by Agostino Tassi, master of perspective architecture, who marked off the spaces of the vault. The subject chosen for the decorations was the glorification of the Ludovisi family by way of heraldic emblems. The ceiling of Cardinal Del Monte's alchemical laboratory, part of the casino, had been decorated in 1597 by Caravaggio, and this is the only work Caravaggio is known to have made in oils on a wall. Prince Antonio Boncompagni Ludovisi added to the building in 1785, but did nothing, however, to alter the splendor of the decorations that Cardinal Ludovico had commissioned from the leading artists of his period. [CVM]

Guercino, *Fame, Honor and Virtue* (1621)

Caravaggio, *Jove, Neptune and Pluto* (1597) >

8 – Palazzo Borghese (16th century)

Piazza della Fontanella di Borghese, 22

The *palazzo* was built in the 14th century based on the design by Jacopo Barozzi known as Vignola, and Cardinal Camillo Borghese – future Pope Paul V (1605-1621), bought it in 1596. The family commissioned Flaminio Ponzio (who had studied Baroque illusionism and scenography) to make changes of enlargement.

The monumental courtyard designed by Carlo Rinaldi with a total of 96 twin columns, is situated at the end of the garden, creating a break with the formal limits of 14th century.

"Il cembalo di Borghese" – "The cymbal of Borghese" so called because of the oblique façade in Via di Ripetta - that precisely looks like a cymbal - is very thin at the top and has a balcony at various levels. While the right side of the building develops in length, with twenty-two windows on three floors.

The main entrance opens wide onto Fontanella di Borghese. From the doorway, which is flanked by two columns with an overhanging balcony with a triangular gable, you enter the courtyard and garden where Rainaldi's nymph, known as the "Bagno di Venere", can be seen.

Paolina Bonaparte, Napoleone's sister and wife of Prince Camillo Borghese sojourned at the Palace. The bigoted Prince did not approve of Paolina's frivolous character, and after much alternation, assigned an apartment to her whereby the only doors communicating with the rest of the *palazzo* were bricked in.

The palazzo is still owned by the Borghese family, but they only inhabit part of it. The rest of the building has been assigned to the offices of the Ambassador of Spain and to the Hunting Club. [AF]

9 – Villa Borghese (17th century)
Piazzale del Museo Borghese

In 1605, when Camillo Borghese, member of an aristocratic Roman family with Sienese origins, was elected pope as Paul V (1605–21), the way was opened for a new era in patronage of the arts, one dominated by a return of gaiety and indulgence. Heir, together with his brothers, to an old piece of property at the Muro Torto, he began buying up the surrounding lots, eventually coming into possession of the extraordinary park that is still without equal in Rome in terms of size and grandeur. Flaminio Ponzio (1560–1613) was commissioned to design the villa, which the pope and

his ambitious nephew Scipione Caffarelli Borghese intended to use for splendid banquets. The Dutch architect and cabinetmaker Giovanni Vasanzio (Jan, or Giovanni, van Santen; ca. 1550–1621) was commissioned to transform the vast, uncultivated grounds into a delightful garden with niches and statues. When Ponzio died, in 1613, Vasanzio took over direction of the work, completing the exterior decoration of the building, which was composed entirely of archaeological relics from the collections of the pope and Scipione as if to announce to visitors the building's true nature as a private museum. The two powerful men were most interested in creating an appropriate setting for their magnificent collection of antiquities, which they assembled with unabated fervor. The decision to use sculpture framed

by stuccowork as decoration for the façade, in keeping with the style employed earlier for the Villa Medici, permitted the use of 70 busts, 43 statues, and 144 bas-reliefs. Each room was named after the most important work of art it contained. When Vasanzio died in 1921, work was almost finished, and Girolamo Rainaldi took his place and the sumptuous gardens were given over to Domenico Savino di Montepulciano.

The celebrated painting collection that is the basis of today's museum dates to the early years of the seventeenth century. Camillo and Scipione dedicated a large portion of their immense wealth to the construction of chapels and monuments. The pope's nephew had an obsessive urge to collect works of art and was capable of even unscrupulous acts to possess them. When

Antonio Canova, *Paolina Borghese* (1804-1808)

Gian Lorenzo Bernini, *David* (1619) >

he could not buy them, he was not above "requisitioning" them. This was the method he employed to confiscate 105 canvases from the unfortunate Cavaliere d'Arpino, who had fallen on hard times after the death of his protector, Pope Clement VII. The works included several by the young Caravaggio. At Scipione's death, in 1633, the trustee overseeing the estate gave the entire property as inheritance to a cousin, Marcantonio II. In these years the *palazzo* was brought to a stage of thorough completion. This state of artistic languor was broken two centuries later under Marcantonio IV, with new works directed by the architect Antonio Asprucci, who radically changed the interior decoration of the villa, giving it the appearance it has today. This period of the last years of the eighteenth century saw the triumph of the neoclassical style with its attendant thirst for all things archaeological. The true apex of this search for ideal nobility is represented by the sublime stateliness of Antonio Canova's marble sculpture of Pauline Borghese as Venus, a work that seems emblematic of the decorations in the rooms.

When Marcantonio died, the villa was inherited by Camillo Borghese, husband of Pauline Bonaparte, and in 1807, after applying much pressure, Napoleon succeeded in convincing his new brother-in-law to sell the marble pieces decorating the villa. In all, 523 pieces left for France, forming the so-called "Borghese Collection" at the Louvre. Fortunately, Bernini's statues were not thought important enough to take; nor was the collection of paintings. The Italian state bought Villa Borghese in 1902, and Vill's museum now houses some of Scipione's extraordinary collection. [CVM]

Caravaggio, *Young Man with Fruit Basket* (1605 ca) >

10 – Palazzo Braschi (18th century)

Piazza San Panteleo, 10

Palazzo Braschi is the last building to be commissioned by a Papal family. The architect Cosimo Morelli carried out the construction at the end of 18th century for the nephew of Pope Pius VI. It was built where the antique Palazzo Orsini stood at the beginning of 1400s. In 1501, Cardinal Oliviero Carafa, as new owner of the *palazzo*, placed a marble torso called Pasquino in the corner of the building. Pasquino became famous for his "pasquinate" - sharp satire aimed against the authorities. Both the common people and the learned would gaze at the torso on its pedestal.

The neoclassical bulk of the *palazzo* clashes with the Baroque harmony of the nearby Piazza Navona. The *palazzo* is trapezoidal with neo 16th century façades on four floors.

The great staircase inside the building is considered to be a jewel of architecture. It was built by Giuseppe Valadier and is enriched by statues, stucco decoration with columns that come from the Hospital of Santo Spirito (which were probably originally from Villa di Agrippina 1st century A.D.) However the Braschi family's fortune was not long lived. During the French occupation in 1798, Pope Pius VI and his nephew Luigi were arrested and taken to France. The *palazzo* was pillaged, the works of art were either stolen or sold. When Luigi returned he was finally able to finish construction on the *palazzo*. When Luigi died in 1816, the *palazzo* went through various owners until the Silvestrelli family sold it to the Italian State.

Palazzo Braschi now houses of the Museum of Rome. [AF]

11 – Palazzo Caetani (16th century)
Via Delle Botteghe Oscure, 32

Alessandro Mattei probabily commissioned Nanni di Baccio Bigio to work on the building in 1564.

In 1682 this solemn expression of late Renaissance architecture became the property of the Negroni family. In 1753 it was sold to the Durazzo family. It was then sold to Cardinal Serbelloni whose heirs, in 1776, sold it to the Caetani family, the Dukes of Sermoneta and Princes of Teano, who were descendents of the family that gave birth to Boniface VIII (1294-1303).

The front façade of the *palazzo* looks out on to Via delle Botteghe Oscure. There are nine windows on each of the three floors. The windows on the upper floor are architraved, while the windows on the mezzanine and ground floor are simply squared. The string-course is embellished by a subtle curved frieze.

There are two courtyards: the first has a portico with a run of three arches, and the second has a fountain decorated by antique fragments.

Taddeo and Federico Zuccari were responsible for the internal decoration of the building in the 15th century. [AF]

12 – Palazzo della Camera di Commercio (17th century)
Piazza di Pietra

In 1871 the Land Customs building, which was constructed on the remains of the Hadrianeum, a temple erected by Antonino Pio in honor of his father Adriano, was given over to the Roman Government by the San Michele Hospice. It was then used for various activities. In 1873 it became the property of the Chamber of Commerce. The building was restructured and adapted to its new function by Virginio Vespignani. The building that Vespignani worked on was the same one that Pope Innocent XII had commissioned Francesco Fontana to transform in 1695. Fontana changed the remains of the temple by uniting the remaining eleven columns into the center of the building, and by creating two wings that were lower than the rest of the building. He also put in three orders of architraved windows between the columns.

Vespignani eliminated any hint of the Baroque, and completely re-did the perspectives on Via de' Burro, the main entrance and the side entrance. The renovation of the antique building started in 1881 and 1882: the columns were separated, the last four were freed in 1928. In the mid twenties, Tullio Passarelli presented his project. It was approved by the Superintendent of Public Works on 28 May 1925. Passarelli introduced a triple arcade in Via de' Burro, scanned by couples of columns. The trabeation and the attic were also added out. The greatest changes were made when he re-proposed smooth capitals, similar to those of Fontana, which Vespignani had replaced with Corinthian capitals. [AF]

13 – Palazzo della Cancelleria (15th century)
Piazza della Cancelleria, 3

To the side of the great theater of Pompey, just to the north of the barracks for one of the squadrons of charioteers that served the circus games, a primitive center of religious worship known as the *titlus* arose early in the Christian era. In the fourth century, Pope Damasus I (364–84) enlarged this structure with the addition of a church in memory of the martyrdom of San Lorenzo. A building was constructed to the side of this to house the Sacred Books of the Roman church. A millennium later, toward the end of the fifteenth century, this *palazzo* came to occupy a central place in the large-scale plans for renewing the city of Rome devised by Pope Sixtus IV, who hoped to restore Rome to its former glory. The stately shape of the *palazzo* fit with the ambitious plans of reconstruction. As indicated by recent archaeological excavations in the courtyard, the *palazzo* covered only partially the site of the ancient temple, which faced a different direction and was a different size, but had been incorporated in the *palazzo* by Riario, making the largest, most impressive, and most highly refined in fifteenth-century Rome. Raffaele Riario received the use, for all his natural life, of the contiguous *palazzo*, which he immediately set about modernizing. The destruction of the older building and the church itself began in 1484, and according to an inscription on the façade the work was

completed in 1495. The final decorations were completed in 1511. He rebuilt the Palazzo of San Damaso, had the church incorporated into the building itself, following the precedent of the Palazzo Venezia, as though it were a Palatine chapel. An anecdote narrated in the Diario of Stefano Infessura recounts how the cardinal won the sum of 14,000 ducats from Franceschetto Cybo playing dice and how, when the pope instructed him to give the money back to the loser, he explained that he could not, since he had already spent it all on wood, bricks, and stone for the construction of the building. The façade, entirely covered in travertine with its floors marked off by rows of classical pilasters, was completed in 1495. The main portal was radically changed in 1589 according to plans by Domenico Fontana. Vasari gives credit to the theory that Bramante was entrusted with the technical supervision of the work, acting in the role of advisor, but the art historian Frommel convincingly attributes the work to Baccio Pontelli (1450-ca. 1494). The rooms were decorated by artists of the calibre of Francesco Salviati, Perin del Vaga and Vasari. The *palazzo* experienced a new period of glory during the early years of the eighteenth century thanks to the theater (no longer in existence) that Filippo Juvarra (1678–1736) designed for Cardinal Pietro Ottoboni, creating a special place for musical performances. On February 9, 1849, the Roman Republic was proclaimed from the *palazzo*. In accordance with the Lateran Treaty, the Cancelleria enjoys extraterritorial status. [CVM]

14 – Castel Sant'Angelo (15th century)

Lungotevere Castello

The emperor Hadrian (A.D. 76–138) was a man of great learning and fore-sight, interested in such diverse subjects as archaeology, philosophy, math-ematics, and, in particular, architecture. For the site for his tomb, Hadrian chose an area on the right bank of the Tiber River, opposite the Campus Martius which he connected to the Campus Martius by way of a new bridge, the Pons Aelius.

The monument, known as Hadrian's Mausoleum or Hadrian's Mole and today part of Castel Sant'Angelo, was inaugurated in 139. It was built in accordance with the three-tier design of early Italian and Roman tra-dition, the same design that had been used earlier for the tomb of Augus-tus. Its three tiers included a broad podiumlike base, atop which stood the main drum, the mausoleum proper, containing the funerary cham-ber, which in turn was topped by a smaller pedestal and drum. The vast funerary chamber was located at the center of the main drum and was reached by way of a spiral ramp. The chamber itself contained the remains of Hadrian, his wife, Sabina, his adopted son, L. Aelius Caesar, and later emperors, the last of whom was Caracalla, killed in A.D. 217. In 271, the emperor Aurelian incorporated the monument as a bastion in the famous walls he had built around the city. The Mausoleum was thus gradually transformed into a fearsome castle protected by the warrior archangel Michael. By the end of the fourth century, the tomb had become a bridge-head fortress. In 590 Rome was struck by plague, and Pope Gregory I (590–604) led a penitential procession through the city to pray for its cessation, during which he saw a vision of the archangel Michael sheath-ing his sword in the air over Hadrian's tomb. A chapel was then built on the tomb, and its name eventually changed to Castel Sant'Angelo.

During the closing centuries of the Middle Ages the castle passed into the hands of powerful noble families, and Pope Nicholas III (1277–80) had the covered passageway built that connects St. Peter's to Castel Sant'An-gelo. At the end of the Babylonian captivity, the various conditions imposed on the citizens of Rome included surrender of the castle, which thus, in 1377, finally became papal property. It was during those years that the

building lost its marble facing. The main drum with the funerary chamber was also strategically set back, surrounded by walkways built around the structure.

Pope Paul III (1534–49) had the greatest impact on the interior decoration, planning the spectacular papal apartment on the upper floor that still bears his name (Pauline). He sought the assistance of Antonio da Sangallo the Younger.

Under his rule, Raffaello da Montelupo was commissioned to make an angel to stand atop the castle to replace the one destroyed in the sack of 1527 (Raffaello's statue was in turn replaced in 1753). And in gold letters he had inscribed on the ceiling of the Sala Paolina, "Everything that is within this fortress, once crumbling, inaccessible, and defaced, now, by merit of Pope Paul III, has been restored, put back in order, and decorated to create enduring strength, commodious use, and subtle elegance." [CVM]

Perin del Vaga, *The Stories of Rome* and *The Storie of Alexander the Great* >

15 – Palazzo Chigi Odescalchi (17th century)

Piazza Santi Apostoli, 80-81

The magnificent *palazzo* that was built opposite the Church of the Santi Apostoli has seen many changes over time, changes in its appearance, but also changes in its name in accordance with the succession of families that, whether because of fate or papal munificence, lived in it and sought to affirm their social status by the splendid architectural work they lavished on it. The original building was the property of the Colonna princes, unrivaled rulers of this quarter of the city. Little remains today of that structure, which was probably turreted, for its appearance changed over time in keeping with the rank and riches of its successive owners.

The building experienced its first complete overhaul at the hands of Carlo Maderno after 1622, when ownership of the building passed from the Colonna family to the Ludovisi Cardinal Ludovico Ludovisi nonetheless left his mark on the structure. He turned to his favorite architect, Maderno, who designed the large courtyard, which has stood unchanged through all subsequent transformations. The arcades were decorated by numerous statues, including two, representing the late emperors Julian and Maximianus, that have survived to today. In 1628, Cardinal Ludovisi sold the *palazzo* back to the Colonna princes, who, in 1657, gave it to members of the up-and-coming Chigi family from Siena.

Interested in having the façade of the *palazzo* reworked, the pope's nephew Mario chose Bernini's proposal, the sketches for which were prepared by Bernini's brother Luigi and Carlo Fontana, effective designer of the work since he was at that time head architect of the Bernini workshop. A document of February 7, 1664, attests to the presence on the site of the great Bernini himself, but his presence in the city of Rome was soon interrupted by his journey to France to present his plans for the Louvre.

In 1746, when the Chigis moved into a new home in Piazza Colonna, the *palazzo* opposite the Church of the Santi Apostoli was bought by Prince Baldassare Odescalchi, great-grandson of Innocent XI (1676–91). In 1750 he commissioned Nicolò Salvi and Luigi Vanvitelli to enlarge the *palazzo* and give it some new luster. To better compete with the Colonna family, whose property stood on the opposite side of the piazza, the two archi-

tects elongated the façade, undoing Bernini's design. They added two doors in the wings at the sides, each door crowned by a balcony and a coat of arms—four bands of silver accompanied by a lion, six incense holders, and a crowned eagle.

Most of the sumptuous furnishings designed for the *palazzo* have been lost. Also gone are the paintings and sculpture, and the tapestries made after designs by Giulio Romano and Peter Paul Rubens that decorated the apartments of Prince Livio early in the eighteenth century, apartments later inhabited by Queen Mary Casimir, widow of John III of Poland, during her visit to Rome. Gone, too, is Cardinal Chigi's spectacular bed, designed by the German painter Johann Paul Schor and covered in white satin painted with floral motifs. The Genoese painter Giovanni Battista Gaulli (1639–1709) also worked here, narrating on the walls of an alcove a *Fable of Endymion* now in Palazzo Chigi in Piazza Colonna. There is also a painting by Caravaggio showing the *Conversion of Paul*, which came to Rome by way of the inheritance of the Genoese collection of Balbi of Piovera.

A fire that destroyed much of the upper floor of the building in 1887 led to the *palazzo*'s most recent transformation. Raffaele Ojetti was commissioned to design a new façade for the Odescalchi property on Via del Corso, and he created the rusticated facade we see today. Its design, very much in keeping with the eclectic trends of those years, is based on a neo-Renaissance Florentine style. [CVM]

16 – Casina delle Civette (20th century)

Villa Torlonia, Via Nomentanta, 70

It was built around 1840 by Giuseppe Jappelli, who had been assigned to project a series of buildings in the park of Villa Torlonia. The current aspect is due to the three different interventions the project underwent. In 1840 Jappelli designed it like a Swiss hut; in 1908 Prince Giovanni Torlonia decided to live there and assigned the architect Gennari to enlarge it, giving it the effect of a medieaval building. In the end in 1916-1920 the architect Vincenzo Fasolo, added a loggia, porticos, fireplaces, small domes, capitals and old fragments of marble and enriched it by using decorative elements like grotesque masks, vases, alegorical statues: a mixture of styles between Medieval and Art Deco. The presence of the multititude of various decorative elements with reference to the owl determined the name by which the building is to this day known.

In 1939 when the Prince died the small villa was abandoned and left to decay. It was temporarily occupied by Anglo-American military forces from 1947 to 1949. In 1978 the entire complex of Villa Torloni was bought by the Town Hall of Rome.

In 1992 restoration started and today it is the seat of The Glass Museum. The Museum contains works by Cesare Picchiarini, which is based on well known artists like Duilio Cambellotti. Many of the works at the villa are by Duilio Cambellotti, including the furniture, the designs and the cartoon preparations. [AF]

17 – Palazzo Del Collegio Romano (16th century)

Piazza del Collegio Romano, 4

Pope Gregorius XIII had Palazzo Del Collegio Romano built in 1582 so as to house the new seat of the Collegio della Compagnia di Gesù.

The great complex, which occupies an area of around 13.000 m², also incorporates the Church of Sant'Ignazio. For many years the *palazzo* was considered to be the work of Bartolomeo Ammannati, but it appears that it was really the work of the Jesuit priest Giuseppe Valeriani.

The majestic tripartite façade presents two monumental doors with the Boncompagni family shield in the center, while the sides of the doors have a series of three windows.

In 1789 an astronomical observation tower was built onto the right side of the building. Carlo Pietrangeli writes that "until 1925 it was a characteristic of old Rome to drop a wicker ball down a six meter long beam, at 12 o'clock sharp, onto the rooftop of the observation tower. This was the given signal for the firing of the Gianicolo cannon".

In 1879, the complex, that is, the Jesuit University and other illustrious cultural institutions (the library, the Kircheriano Museum and the astronomical observatory), were all taken away with the exception of the Church of Sant'Ignazio.

Initially it was to house the Senate of the Kingdom, but the bulk of the work necessary to adapt it for this use was too much. So Palazzo Madama was chosen instead.

In December 1870 the right wing was given over to the first state school of the Kingdom of Rome. Prior to that it had been used as a barracks. [AF]

18 – Palazzo Colonna (17th-18th centuries)

Piazza SS. Apostoli, 66

The Colonna family, descendents of the Counts of Tuscolo who dominated the city around the year 1000, had for centuries been the baronial protagonists of the struggle against the Papacy. Martin V (1417-1431) restructured the *palazzo*, built on the antique construction ruined by Boniface VIII. During the 1600s the Colonna family united all their property in order to erect a *palazzo* worthy of their family lineage.

The structure, worked on by Antonio Del Grande and Girolama Fontana, but concluded by Nicola Michetti in 1730, was developed at right angles around the main courtyard. Even if, according to Ravaoglioli, the external design of the *palazzo* was quite modest, the sumptuous dimensions of the internal decoration made up for it. In the 18th century the *palazzo* was almost completely restructured.

What has remained, though, are the famous stories of the parties that the Colonna family held. Guests would be invited and obliged to "have a pee" in elegant vases that were adorned with myrtle and twigs of orange, before they were allowed into the main hall.

The *palazzo* was home to Lodovico il Bavaro and Petrarch and then to the poetess Vittoria Colonna, friend of Michelangelo, and Marc'Antonio victorious of the battle of Lepanto.

In this *palazzo* on the night of 4th June 1802, Charles Emanuel IV of Savoy, King of Sardinia, dethroned by Napoleon, abdicated in favor of his brother Victor Emanuel I, and then joined the Jesuit order.

The art gallery, built by Antonio Del Grande, is the only open public space of the building. From the gallery one can admire the private garden of the *palazzo*. [AF]

19 – Palazzo dei Conservatori (15th-16th centuries)

Piazza del Campidoglio, 1

Since the mythic age of Romulus and Remus the Capitoline Hill has been the heart of Rome. The hill was damaged by fires many times in antiquity, necessitating several reconstructions. Each of these projects was followed by an even larger one, every one of them, as Cassiodorus wrote, "exceeding the capacity of human ingenuity." Abandonment, however, came with the fall of Rome. During the pontificate of Paul III the decision was made to radically transform the chaotic assembly of battlemented structures in this area. The transformation of this zone began in the first days of 1538 with the transfer of the monumental bronze equestrian statue of Emperor Marcus Aurelius from its original position near St. John Lateran to the center of Piazza Campidoglio. Years were to pass before, in 1562, Michelangelo finally undertook construction of the façade of the Palazzo dei Conservatori, opposite which he decided to put a twin structure, the Palazzo Nuovo. Even though Michelangelo died before completing this project, those who followed him remained faithful to his instructions, at least in terms of the general layout. He was replaced by one of his pupils, Giacomo della Porta, who, except for a few modifications, followed the directives of the great master. By the end of 1580, the façade of the Palazzo dei Conservatori had been finally completed.

The original *palazzo*, built during the fifteenth century at the request of Nicholas V, had not been demolished but simply restored and updated in accordance with contemporary canons. The portico had been used as the setting for the first sculptures of the Capitoline collection, founded by Sixtus IV in 1471 (considered the first public museum of classical sculpture since antiquity), including statues of river divinities, the She -Wolf, emblem of the city, and the *Spinario*. The halls on the *piano nobile*, frescoed in the fifteenth and sixteenth centuries by such artists as Jacopo Ripando with the stories of ancient Rome, were reached by way of an austere, monumental stairway designed by Michelangelo. Several rooms were decorated during the first half of the 1540s. The great Sala degli Orazi e dei Curiazi, decorated by Giuseppe Cesari, the artist best known as Cavaliere d'Arpino (1568–1640), presented a series of *Histories of Ancient*

Rome. In the seventeenth century, Bernini and Alessandro Algardi set the two gigantic statues of their benefactors, Urban VIII and Innocent X, at the sides of the great hall.

Miraculously spared damage during the many and various periods of destruction during our times, the Piazza Campidoglio and the Palazzo dei Conservatori remain emblematic of the history of Rome. The buildings on the piazza designed by Michelangelo are today the headquarters of the city's picture collection and archaeological collection, including the original statue of Marcus Aurelius. [CVM]

20– Palazzo della Consulta (18th century)
Piazza del Quirinale, 41

Pope Clement XII (1730-1740) had the *palazzo* built. It was destined to house the "Sacra Consulta" courts where civil and criminal law would be practised, along with two small military corps, their living quarters and stables. The *palazzo* was built in order to embellish the nearby Palazzo del Quirinale which was being finished at the same time. Between 1732 and 1737 the building was constructed over the ruins of the thermal baths of Constantine. The ruins were made use of for the foundation of the *palazzo*, in accordance with Ferdinando Fuga's project.

Fuga offers an example of the most elegant monument, where the visual rhythm of the *palazzo* is broken by exquisite groups of sculptures above

the three doorways with an almost virtuoso warble resembling the aspirations of the European royalty. The urbanistic "behind the scenes" perspective of the space of the piazza, is completely freed of the façade where, at ground level the ashlar work fades into a thin engraved strip within a framework of simple bands around which two sets of triangularly arched windows are aligned. It is noteworthy how the central body of the building widens and, gable free, merges into the prevailing horizontal lines of the partitions. The halls are decorated with frescoes by Antonio Bicchierai, Giovan Domenico Piastrini and Liborio Coccetti. In 1798 Napoleon stayed at the *palazzo* during the French occupation of Rome, it was then taken over by the prefecture of the city and then it became the residence of heirs of Prince Humbert and Princess Margaret of Savoy. [AF]

21 – Quartiere Coppedè (20th century)
Via Dora: Piazza Mincio and surrounding area

In the post-War period, Rome was experiencing a severe housing shortage, due mainly to an increase in its population. One of the main results was that a vast number of buildings were constructed, without much concern for aesthetic or technical aspects. In the ensuing desolate building panorama, Coppedè might well be defined one of the least worthy architects in Rome's artistic tradition.

The first project for this series of buildings was signed by Gino Coppedè, which included from 18 to 27 buildings varying in size from small hamlets to large villas. The so-called "Ambasciatori" ("Ambassadors") complex took its aesthetic inspiration from the nearby fountain in Piazza Mincio, and comprises three distinct units that have been reunited in two large, triangular blocks which are dissected by Via Diagonale. The large entrance arch constitutes the "triumphal" entrance to the heart of the complex.

Towers, turrets and balconies create a fantasmagorical mix between a castle and a palazzo, with Neo-Mannerist touches added to give the complex some much-needed classical rigour.

The same interpretative language is used for other constructions built in the area between 1917 and 1921. Coppedè's contribution is evident throughout, including the buildings in Piazza Mincio and the group of three villas known as "The Fairy Villas". Those buildings not directly built by Coppedè were built by his main collaborator Paolo Emilio Andrè.

[AF]

22 – Palazzo Doria-Pamphili (16th-17th centuries)
Via del Corso, 304

The *palazzo*'s importance today seems tied more than ever to the magnificent art collection that has been displayed in its enormous gallery since the eighteenth century. Closely tied by two marriages to the Aldobrandini and Doria families, the Pamphili family slowly put together the complex we see today, which can be entered by way of six monumental entrances leading to five courtyards. Prince Camillo Pamphili (1622–1666), nephew of Innocent X, acquired the first holding after returning from a short stay in Avignon as papal legate. To direct the work he called on Antonio del Grande, a follower of Girolamo Rainaldi, and architect of the gallery in Palazzo Colonna. His uncle Innocent X (1644–55) demonstrated little interest in art, but he did commission Velázquez to paint his portrait, today judged perhaps the most beautiful portrait of the seventeenth century and displayed in the gallery. Ownership then passed to the Della Rovere family, who further embellished it before handing it on to Cardinal Pietro Albobrandini, nephew of Clement VIII, in 1601. To decorate a chapel flanking the church, he asked Annibale Carracci to make the celebrated lunettes on canvas that are today preserved in the gallery. The inventory of the Aldobrandini collection, compiled by Monsignor Giovan Battista Agucchi in 1603, documents the extraordinary nucleus of paintings, including Titian's *Salome* and the Este collection of Ferrara paintings. A series of fifteenth century buildings, property of Camillo's wife, thus came to be incorporated into the Palazzo of the Collegio Romano, creating the great complex that still belongs to the family. Camillo's son Benedetto inaugurated a series of rooms around the courtyard dedicated to painting. The Stanza dei Quadri is followed by the Stanza degli Animali and finally the much-loved Stanza dei Paesi, full of sunny landscapes by Claude Lorrain and Gaspard Dughet. Antonio del Grande finished work on the building of the Collegio Romano in 1675.

In 1731, Prince Don Camillo Pamphili asked one of the few representatives of the rococo style in Rome, Gabriele Valvassori, to rebuild the main façade and integrate it by closing off its open loggia. The *palazzo* then took a rich allure, more in harmony with the times. The collection of paintings con-

tinued to grow, thanks to the inheritance that the Genoese Doria family left to the Pamphili. The gallery, covered with Pompeiian decorations by Annibale Angelini, kept up to date with archaeological discoveries.

This opulent *palazzo*, more than any other *palazzo* in Rome, offers the opportunity not just to admire works of art but to experience something of the spirit that led to the formation of the great Roman collections, the majority of which are no longer intact. The Doria Pamphili collection of paintings and sculpture has survived across centuries of history and is open to the public thanks to the farsighted efforts of the heirs. [CVM]

Aureliano Milani, *The feats of Hercules* (1767-1769) >

23 – Casino di Villa Doria Pamphili (17th century)
Via di San Pancrazio

This is probably the most beautiful and well kept villa dating from 17th century Rome. The main part with the cottage and the garden terrace was projected by Alessandro Algardi and Grinmani between 1644 and 1652. They interpreted a Baroque style tempered with a measure of Apollinean and Classic styles.

The villa is also called "Buon Respiro" and was built by order of Camillo Pamphili, nephew to Innocent X who gave the project to Borromini. Borromini put together a plan that is huge and where two long side wings combined with a terrace articulated at different levels, and sumptuously furnished, both internally and externally. Even the garden, which was enlarged by Valvassori in 1730, has precious fountains, statues, prospects of water and a great variety of plants including an enormeus pine tree. [AF]

24 – Palazzo Falconieri (16th-17th centuries)
Via Giulia, 1

The *palazzo*, which had been commissioned by the Odescalchi family, was built in 1576. In 1606 it was bought by the Farnese family, who in 1637 took over the surrounding land owned by Orazio Falconieri. Falconieri was a descendant of a Florentine family who had acquired wealth and influence through having a contract on salt tax. It was at this time that the *palazzo* underwent a period of glory.

In 1646 Francesco Borromini was commissioned by Orazio Falconieri to give unity to and renew the building which still had the Farnese "Lilly" and the heraldic family symbols of the Odescalchi family. The original work by Borromini, however, still maintains its particular style. This can be seen especially in the body of the "L" form, added to the lodge that looks towards the river. The façade that looks onto Via Giulia has a series of decorations, particular to Borromini, like the pilaster strips that end in the form of a falcon's head with a female bust (perhaps a celebration of the beautiful women in the Falconieri family). From the river the best view allows you to see writings in the shape of a Corinthian half-column. By taking "classic" elements, Borromini gives new meaning to architectural language: modeled like a sculpture, the space is shifted and moved by chiaroscuro profiles, whereby the decorative elements are impregnated with a new and vibrant structural sense. Internally, Borromini, a skilful stucco-worker, conceived decorations of extraordinary originality that paved the way for the Rococo.

In 1865 the Falconieri family died out, and the *palazzo* was sold to the Medici del Vascello family. In 1880 on the occasion of work done along the Tiber, the section of the building closest to the Tiber was completely modified. From 1937 the building has been owned by the Hungarian Republic and is seat of the Hungarian Academy. [AF]

Francesco Borromini, Ceiling >

25 – Palazzo Farnese (16th century)

Piazza Farnese, 1

Alessandro Farnese, first as cardinal and then as Pope Paul III (1534–49), built this *palazzo*, its magnificence designed as an unmistakable expression of the dominant role he intended his papacy to play within Roman aristocracy.

Cardinal Alessandro turned to Antonio da Sangallo the Younger. Crystal clear in its structure and truly imposing, the *palazzo* for the Farnese family perfectly expressed Alessandro's solid nobility as a passionate humanist and collector of medallions and marbles, gemstones and coins.

The *palazzo* that Sangallo designed for the cardinal was enlarged and embellished after Alessandro was elected pope as Paul III, in 1534. Following Sangallo's death in 1546 many artists contributed to this transformation, from Vasari to Perino del Vaga and Sebastiano del Piombo. By a twist of fate, in 1547 the pope entrusted the work to Michelangelo, who was a dedicated foe of what he himself derided as the "Sangallo gang." In the Farnese, Michelangelo contributed to the completion of the top floor, making it taller and topping it with a powerful cornice. He designed the arcaded window beside the main entrance and the third order along the

courtyard, for which Sangallo had drawn his inspiration from the decorative system of the Colosseum. The columned atrium designed by Sangallo, as well as the first two orders of the courtyard, reflected Alessandro's classical taste. The beautiful loggia looking out over the Tiber, on the back of the *palazzo*, was designed by Giacomo della Porta.

Francesco Salviati (1510–63) probably began the decoration of the Salotto Dipinto in 1554. The great military commander Alessandro Farnese died

in 1592, leaving the ducal titles to Parma and Piacenca to his first-born son, another Ranuccio. His second-born son, Odoardo, became cardinal at seventeen and set about completing the decoration of the Roman *palazzo*. The double-story Sala Grande, yet to be decorated, gave the young heir the opportunity to continue the glorification of his father begun by Salviati. The artistic panorama of Rome was enriched by the new and decisive presence of Annibale Carracci, who on the invitation of Odoardo moved from

Bologna to take part in the decorations. He began with the cardinal's private *studiolo* in 1595, setting aside the Sala Grande. Pleased with the work the cardinal immediately entrusted Annibale Carracci with the decoration of the ceiling of the gallery, which he worked on with the assistance of his brother Agostino and a large team of assistants, including Domenichino (Domenico Zampieri) and Giovanni Lanfranco. The centerpiece in the middle of the vault is the Triumph of Bacchus and Ariadne, a triumph of profane and sensual love, illustrating the mythical story with the greatest realism. Packed by Odoardo with antique sculptures from the famous Farnese collection, the gallery brought to life a new language, and the *palazzo* was in the vanguard of inventiveness, offering the world a view of the still-nascent baroque style.

After the death, in 1731, of the last Farnese of the Neapolitan line of the Bourbons, the library and archaeological collection were taken to Naples, and the *palazzo* began a slow decline from which it was rescued only in 1874, when it was rented to the ambassador of France. [CVM]

26 – Villa Chigi, known as La Farnesina (16th century)
Via della Lungara, 230

The wealthy Sienese banker Agostino Chigi (c. 1465–1520) selected a spot along the west bank of the Tiber, just outside the walls of the city, as the site for his second residence, a villa in which he planned to lead the life described by the ancients. In 1505, the Sienese painter and architect Baldassare Peruzzi (1481–1536) gave this rural fantasy its exquisitely elegant form. The exterior of the building, today plastered over, was originally covered with monochrome decorations of fairy-tale gaiety composed of telamons and plant elements made by Peruzzi himself. Truly neopagan, both in its intentions and its inspiration, the villa draws much from the celebrated villa of Pliny. Villa Chigi is most famous for its fresco decorations, in particular those made by Raphael and his followers in the loggia connecting the two wings of the villa and overlooking the garden. The garden loggia on the ground floor is decorated with scenes that present, far from any Christian reference, Agostino Chigi's horoscope, skillfully blending mythological figures with the emblems of the Zodiac following the

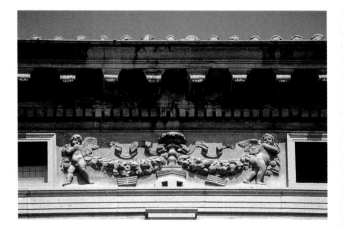

ancient neoplatonic interpretation revised and brought back into fashion by the Tuscan humanist Marsilio Ficino. In the private rooms of this enchanting hide-away the leading artists of the Renaissance met. Their creations attest to Agostino Chigi's cultural ambitions, and as banker to popes from Alexander VI to Leo X, he was the only man with the means to compete with Julius II for the services of the best artists available. These included Peruzzi, of course, and Raphael, who had been working for him since 1510; there was also Sebastiano del Piombo, the great student of Giovanni Bellini, who came all the way from Venice in 1512 to paint the head of the giant Polyphemus. A year later, at the banker's request, Raphael painted a fresco of the Triumph of Galatea to complement Sebastiano's

Giulio Romano, *Three Graces Listening to Psyche* (detail) >

painting. In 1517 Raphael and his best students painted the vault of the entrance loggia, orchestrating the events of Psyche and Cupid—and what background could have been more suitable for the banker's famous love affairs? While Giulio Romano frescoed the scenes with figures from Apuleius' *The Golden Ass*, Giovanni da Udine painted garlands of flowers and fruit.

On the second floor of the villa Peruzzi designed the Sala delle Prospettive, the decoration of which reflects the period's interest in illusionistic painting. This important decorative cycle, made between 1515 and 1517, stands out as a shining example of the surprising talents of this versatile artist. Adjacent to this salon is a bedroom, and for its decoration Chigi turned to the artist known to Vasari as Sodoma. Sodoma finished these frescoes in 1518, the same year that Agostino Chigi married the mistress with whom he had been living for seven years and who ultimately bore him five children.

Despite the central role that Agostino Chigi performed in its creation, the villa today bears the name of Alessandro Farnese, who acquired it in 1579. By then, La Farnesina, as it is also known, had slowly fallen into decay, but the cardinal endeavored to revive it and had the fresco decorations finished in the Sala della Galatea. Reduced in size and disfigured, with much of the area of its magnificent garden stolen away, the villa today is but a shadow of its former self. Gone is the famous loggia open onto the Tiber where Agostino held banquets overlooking the trees and the river. Representative of a rich and cultured middle class, he wanted to create a place for satisfying mind and body, far from every outward manifestation of power. That spirit still emanates from what remains of this magic place. [CVM]

Sebastiano del Piombo, *The Fall of Phaeton* (circa 1512) >

27 – Farnesina ai Baullari (16th century)

Corso Vittorio Emanuele II, 168

Tommaso Le Roy, British Prelate, who arrived in Rome in 1494, following the King of France Charles VIII, commissioned the building. Subsequently Francis I, in order to recompense him for the advice given in the agreement with Leo X, declared him "nobile" – a nobleman - and granted to unite his family shield, which was the figure of an ermine, with the Lilies of France. The *palazzo* received its name due to this ambiguity generated by the "Lilies", which adorned the string-course strips bands in view and which became exchanged for the heraldic lilies of the Farnesina family. The construction started in 1523, according to many, based on a project by Antonio da Sangallo il Giovane, and it is one of the best examples of Roman Renaissance architecture. It was heavily damaged during the sack of Rome in 1527, but Raoul Le Roy, nephew to the Prelate, restored and furnished it sumptuously. The building has often been manhandled, and the view onto Corso Vittorio Emanuele II is an imitation and was finished around 1904 by Enrico Guj. The original 15th century façade can be found on Vicolo dell'Aquila: on the ground floor with its ashlar work, there is a four windowed doorway with radial ashlar work which has small square windows beneath it. While on the upper floors, divided by an ample string-course strip decorated with lilies and ermines, centered arched triangular windows alternate. During some restoration work they came across a courtyard with a portico which had a decoration of 14th century figures on it. One of the figures showed a cavalier running after his horse. It is thought that the stables for the fourth faction of the circus had its stables here. The four factions were: Albata, Prasina, Russata and Veneta. Subsequently the *palazzo* was rented and then sold until the last owners, the Baldassarri family, sold it to the Town Hall of Rome in 1885.

Since 1948 it has been the seat of the Barracco Museum. Great works of art are housed here, including Egyptian, Assyrian, Greek, Etruscan and Roman pieces – all donated to the Town Hall of Rome by Giovanni Barracco. [AF]

28 – Palazzo Gaddi (16th century)

Via del Banco di Santo Spirito, 42

During the Papal reign of Clement VII, Cardinal Gaddi commissioned Jacopo Sansovino to restructure what had once been a modest house on Via del Banco di Santo Spirito and turn in into the family *palazzo* in 1530. Michelangelo lived there in 1544 and in 1546. It was also home to Benvenuto Cellini, who, fleeing from Rome after being accused of murdering a jeweler, left arms and precious objects with the Gaddi family. Annibal Caro, the poet, also lived there and a bust of his can be found in the vestibule. Near the *palazzo* the Sienese banker, Agostino Chigi, who apparently kept the papal tiara for years as a pawn exchange for a debit made by Pope Julius II, opened his first bank there.

The *palazzo* still has the original 15th century form and was the last work to be made by the Roman Sansovino. The refined disposition of the plan with its double courtyard, which houses an important array of antique marbles, with niches adorned with statues and cornices decorated by friezes festooned and masqued, they are all themes frequent in the mannerist architecture particular to Northern Italy. It is said that once there was a sculptured group showing Mars and Venus, works by Simone Moschino. They were considered so "daring" that they were initially covered up, and then they went missing.

One characteristic of the *palazzo* is the beautiful spacious 15th century lodge that looks towards a opening in front of Palazzo della Zecca.

In the 1600s the Bandini family owned the building, then it was passed on to Valdina Cremona and on to the Nicolini family. At the beginning of the 1800s it was bought by the Amici family who restored it in 1841.

[AF]

29 – Villa Giulia (16th century)

Piazzale di Villa Giulia, 9

In 1550, a year of jubilee, Cardinal Giovanni Maria del Monte was elected Pope Julius III (1550–55), and he began work on his ambitious projects right away. He directed most of his efforts to building and embellishing Villa Giulia just beyond the city walls.

From the very beginning, three well-known architects—Ammanati, Vasari, and Vignola—gravitated around the pope, and even the great Michelangelo himself is mentioned in a Florentine document according to which "nothing was done without the advice of Buonarroti." The absence of an overall plan and the mingling of so many different artists in the effort makes

it difficult to assess the history of the villa's construction. We do know, how-ever, that Giacomo da Vignola (1507–1573) eventually became Julius III's favorite architect. It was Vignola who began work on the construction of a simple *palazzo* whose somber walls concealed the delights of a worldly court.

The courtyard, enclosed by a broad semicircular portico, provided the orig-inal spatial layout for the main body of the villa. The ground floor was frescoed by the celebrated workshop directed by Taddeo Zuccaro. Another courtyard led from the villa to the theatrical nymphaeum, by Amma-nati, a lively and joyous setting with walls originally covered by precious marbles, hammered metals, and an opulent profusion of gold and stuccoes that descended all the way to the grotto below. This was the center of the villa, and also its most heavily decorated spot. The loggia of the nymphaeum was completed by the end of 1553.

Quick-tempered and somewhat blunt, Julius III attracted more than his share of enemies, and after his death, in 1555, his beloved villa was mer-cilessly sacked. The pope's home was stripped of furnishings, its aviaries were emptied, statues stolen, bubbling fountains shut off. Over the cen-turies, it became a storage dump for agricultural implements.

Now open to the public as the seat of an Etruscan museum, the Villa Giulia has, following restoration of those portions that survived, a new dig-nity. But its appearance for the most part does not convey the grandiose plans of the man who first envisioned it. [CVM]

The cupola decorations undertaken by Federico and Taddeo Zuccaro >

30 – Palazzo del Laterano (16th century)

Piazza San Giovanni in Laterano, 6

The *palazzo*, which originally goes back to the era of Constantine, was the first Papal seat, the so called "Patricarchio"or the real *palazzo* of Christianity where all the important matters of the Church took place until the captivity of Avignon. It was demolished by order of Pope Julius III, because it was deemed unsafe. The building was restructured by Domenico Fontana in 1586 as commissioned by Sextus V, the "the hard Pope" as he was nicknamed by the poet Giuseppe Gioachino Belli.

The *palazzo* was built as part of an urban-architectural project, which considered Rome to be "caput mondi", and it was constructed in a very short time and at reduced costs. This was partly due to the cheap manpower and because the materials used were taken from ruins nearby. One side of the *palazzo* leans against the Basilica the an other three repeat the same ornamental and structural motifs, which denote the obvious aspiration to Palazzo Farnese. That is: windows that are placed on two floors that alternate centered triangular arches and a crowned moulding, with a heraldic frieze. On the east side of Piazza San Giovanni in Laterano there is a building that was also built by Fontana, that contains the only two remaining parts of the antique Palazzo del Laterno: the Sanctum Sanctorum, the Pope's private chapel and the Scala Santa of 28 steps considered to be the stairs that Christ took to go to Pontius Pilate during the trial.

The *palazzo* was conceived as the Papal summer residence, but it has always remained without a clear destination. It has been used as the residence for the Canons of the Lateran Basilica, an hospital for orphans, an archive for the Papal State, a museum for ethnological missionaries, until John XXXIII decided to make it the seat of Vicarship for the Diocese of Rome.

A general restoration took place and ended in 1967 by order of Paul VI. It has finally been restored to it full splendor. [AF]

31 – Palazzo Madama (16th century)
Piazza Madama, 11

The *palazzo* was named after Margaret of Austria in Italian, known as Madama Margherita d'Austria, the illegitimate daughter of the Emperor Charles V, and widow to Alessandro de'Medici from whom she inherited the *palazzo*.

It was built in the 16th century for the Medici family. Cosimo the Elder possibly founded a branch of his Florentine bank in the *palazzo*, and it was the residence of the two Medici Cardinals Giovanni and Giuliano who respectively became Pope Leo X and Pope Clement VII.

The granddaughter of Pope Clement VII, Caterina de' Medici, the grim heroin of the slaughter of the Huguenots, lived at the *palazzo* in 1533 before marrying Henry, son of François I the King of France.

In order to construct the *palazzo* is was necessary to knock down the ruins of the thermal baths of the Neronian or Alexandrian era, and it rises partially on the mediaeval houses of the Crescenzi family. A tower has remained stuck in one of the most recent constructions.

The architect of this building with its 15th century form with three floors and a grand central courtyard, has remained unknown. The actual Baroque façade (mid 17th century) is the work of Ludovico Cardi da Cigoli and Paolo Marucelli. The *palazzo* presents a main doorway, characterized by the original decoration of the skin of a lion and two series of windows with the mezzanine adorned at the gable by a grand lily – the Farnese family symbol – and a rich sculptural decoration.

The *palazzo* has housed the Italian Senate since 1871.

In 1926 to 1929 the *palazzo* was connected to the nearby Palazzo Carpegna and in 1931 it was demolished and the façade facing Via della Dogana Vecchia was restructured. It was connected below street level with the *palazzo* in front of it, which is Palazzo Giustiniani, the private residency of the President of the Senate. [AF]

32 – Villa Madama (16th century)
Via di Villa Madama, 1

Villa Madama, designed by Raphael for Cardinal Giulio de' Medici and celebrated as one of the first modern re-creations of a Roman country villa, has suffered a fate fully as harsh and tormented as that of its original owner. When he was elected pope as Clement VII (1523–34) he was forced to witness firsthand the break-up of the humanist dream and the culminating moment of that collapse, the ferocious sack of Rome in 1527 at the hands of the mercenary troops of Charles V. Originally planned as a work without equal, capable of handing on to posterity the towering grandeur of the Medici family, the villa has barely survived and no longer even bears a Medici name.

Work on the villa began under Raphael's direct supervision in the last months of 1518; but as with other commissions, he was soon joined by

his pupils. Raphael envisioned a series of rooms, at different levels extending across the hillside down to the river, that would together form a large complex. These rooms were designed for large-scale receptions, splendid celebrations for foreign diplomats. Guests were to be welcomed at a garden terrace with a semicircular theater, based on ancient Roman theaters. Fish ponds, stables with space for up to four hundred horses, and all accommodations were nearby to delight them and meet their every need, whether physical or spiritual. The villa's layout included rooms designed to serve certain purposes according to the season, some offering relief from summer heat, others providing shelter in the winter.

A very general sense of Raphael's original plan can be gleaned from surviving documents, but the great many changes made during the course of the actual construction work created a gulf between the original plan and the final creation. Unfortunately the frescoes are now in a poor state of preservation, and very little remains of the giant with infants and satyrs playing about him.

Antonio da Sangallo the Younger actively participated in the creation of the villa, most probably as of technical adviser.

Work on the villa was interrupted by the death of Leo X. Not long afterward, during the sack of Rome in 1527, the mercenary soldiers eager to hang Clement VII destroyed much of the villa. The magnificent loggia, its monumental bays opening onto the garden, still stands.

Having survived the threat to his life, the pope soon arranged two astute marriages: that of his niece Catherine de' Medici to the second-born son of the king of France and that of Alessandro de' Medici to Margaret, known as Madama, the illegitimate daughter of Emperor Charles V. It is for this young woman, although she made no contribution to it, that the villa is named. Thus what was meant to be the most celebrated Roman villa of the sixteenth century was destined to become a simple hayloft. Never completed, devastated, and then restored, the villa survives as a pale shadow of its original plans. [CVM]

The decorative frieze by Giulio Romano >

33 – Palazzo Massimo alle Colonne (16th century)
Corso Vittorio Emanuele II, 141

The Massimo family traces its lineage farther back through the centuries than any other Roman family, claiming an uninterrupted line that begins with the origin of the city itself. The family's fortified home, thrown together with medieval disorder and built upon later, was destroyed in 1527 during the terrible sack of Rome that threw its dark shadow over the towering ideals of humanism.

A few years later, the Sienese architect Baldassare Peruzzi was commissioned to reconstruct the central *palazzo*, and his work on this building came to represent the greatest expression of his architectural skills.

The building stands on the site of the ancient odeon, a theater for musical contests, of the emperor Domitian, and its façade follows the semi-

circular curve of the ancient building's *cavea*. For the Massimo *palazzo* Peruzzi drew on his entire repertory of ideas gleaned from ancient ruins, including those he had studied firsthand. The wonderful portico, decorated with elegant stuccowork and supported by the six Doric columns that give the *palazzo* its name (*alle Colonne*), leads to the first courtyard, which recreates the Vitruvian model of the *vestibulum*. Peruzzi was forced to resort to some odd expedients in his efforts to preserve as much as possible of the damaged original building. He maintained existing walls in an attempt to hold down costs. The dark vestibule, covered by a barrel vault decorated with stuccoes and bas-reliefs, was probably made after Peruzzi's death in 1536 by the members of his workshop. Inexpensive materials were used with exquisite dexterity, and in an obsessive effort to reconstruct the ancient past, Peruzzi planned a dining room for the ground floor and indicated it on his designs as a triclinium. A century later, Carlo Camillo Massimo installed a small nymphaeum built to replace the original ancient fountain. The second courtyard, most of which dates to the seventeenth century, preserves the sole surviving element of the ancient odeon, mixed in among the collection of various other "curiosities" that the Massimos, like most Renaissance families, collected. A stairway adorned by marble relics led up to the frescoed loggia of the first floor, right up to the threshold of a door crowned by the coat-of-arms of the Massimo family. The Palazzo di Pirro, built for Pietro's brother Angelo, was connected to the rebuilt Palazzo del Portico.

In the great hall Daniele da Volterra made frieze decorations of the life of the legendary Fabius Maximus, and Perino del Vaga covered the walls of the side rooms with grotesques and scenes taken from the *Aeneid*.

The urban fabric of the little piazza behind the *palazzo* is still intact, as is the Massimo family's Palazzetto Istoriato, with its façade decorated with monochrome frescoes by Polidoro da Caravaggio; it, too, is connected to the two *palazzos* that the brothers Piero and Angelo built. The exterior decoration presents scenes of the marriage of the Virgin, the life of Esther, and the murder of Holofernes. Mail coaches and couriers once set off from this piazza on routes leading even to foreign countries, part of a service directly related to the Massimo family, since a Massimo was postmaster general of the pontifical post in the eighteenth century. [CVM]

34 – Villa Medici (16th century)
Viale Trinità dei Monti

From its very beginning, Villa Medici was meant to be marvelous; it was a home built to enchant and to astonish. Cardinal Giovanni Ricci of Montepulciano (1497–1574), a wealthy and powerful Tuscan, put antique sculptures and parrots, slaves and Moors within its walls, bringing splendor and life back to places imbued with classical memories. Such classical allusions were appropriate for the Pincian Hill in the northeastern area of the city, the site of the celebrated villa of Lucullus, which with the passing of the centuries had fallen into ruin.

Immediately after acquiring a small holding from the Crescenzi family, Cardinal Ricci called on Nanni di Baccio Bigio (c. 1512–1568), who had already worked for him on a Vatican apartment and in his *palazzo* in

Via Giulia. Giovanni Ricci died in 1574, and two years later the villa passed into the hands of Ferdinando de' Medici. The Medici's official architect, Bartolomeo Ammanati, was summoned to adapt the central body of the villa, to beautify the garden, and in general to add splendor and elegance to this new Medici property. Ammanati designed the beautiful spiral stairway and enlarged the vestibule on the ground floor to create a truly monumental entrance way. Ancient columns made of polychrome marble were set up in the great hall leading to the loggia. The Villa's art collection once also included a *Madonna* by Raphael and numerous works by Andrea del Sarto, Pontormo, Salviati, and others.

Ferdinando, for his secret meetings with his lover, Clelia Farnese, had a small apartment built near the Aurelian walls. It was decorated to create

a kind of pavilion and its vaults were frescoed by Jacopo Zucchi with plant and animal motifs.

In 1587, when, as heir, Ferdinando de' Medici became in his turn grand duke and left Rome for Florence, the villa began a slow decline into neglect. Thus began the dark years that ended with the transfer of the painting collection to the Pitti palace in Florence under Grand Duke Cosimo III. Gian Gastone, the last Medici, undertook restoration work to consolidate the villa, but at his death, in 1737, ownership passed to the house of Lorraine. The archaeological collection was moved to Florence in 1770. When the Academy of France decided to move its headquarters from Palazzo Mancini on the Via del Corso to the Pincian Hill, a new period of glory began for the magnificent home.

It was during the reign of Louis XIV that the habit of seeking artists in Italy began to wane and the supremacy that Italian artists had so long enjoyed in foreign courts began to weaken. French artists grew more sure of themselves, and hostility toward Italian painting increased. In 1666, with the full support of the Sun King himself, the decision was made to create a French academy in Rome to make it possible for French art students to share the great opportunity Italian students had to study firsthand the masterpieces of the past. Colbert, Le Brun, and Bernini provided early impetus to the Académie de France, which holds competitions and then rewards the winners with the opportunity to live and study in Rome. The academy came back to life during the period of the Consulate, at which time the decision was made to move the main building to the Villa Medici on the Pincian Hill. An important period thus began for both the villa and the academy. Large-scale construction projects were undertaken, with classrooms and apartments set up in the gardens; and new areas of study, including music and engraving, were added to those already covered by the academy. In 1961, Malraux, then France's Minister for Culture, nominated the painter Balthus to be director general, and under Balthus further initiatives were undertaken, including the addition of new areas of study, such as filmmaking and photography, and the organization of exhibitions and concerts. [CVM]

35 –Palazzo Medici Lante (16th century)
Piazza Dei Caprettari, 70

In 1513 Leo X commissioned Jacopo Sansovino to build the *palazzo* for his brother Giuliano de Medici. When Giuliano died in 1516, the *palazzo* was passed on to Marantonio Palsoi in 1533 and, still incomplete, it was bought in 1558 by Ludovico Lante who completed it and hung his name on the beam over the main entrance. At the beginning of 1600s Cardinal Marcello Lante assigned Onorio Longhi to follow through some work and during the second half of the 1700s, it was restored by order of Cardinal Federico Marcello Lante by the architect Carlo Murena. In 1873 the *palazzo* was passed on, after the death of Guilio Lante, to his daughter Caterina. It later became the property of the Guglielmi family and finally it was taken over by the Aldobrandini family, who still own it.

The building, with its, 1500s form has a feeling of the work of Bramante and Raffaello. The monumental façade is horizontally marked by two string-course frames based on which, there are architraved windows on corbels and overhanging small square windows. On the second floor there are architraved windows and on the third floor the windows have a simple frame. Sansovino gained much from his work in the courtyard. Though today it has changed due to the closure of the porticos and the loggia, from which 10 columns seemed to have come from the Coliseum while the capitals and the family shields are definitely works by Sansovino. [AF]

36 – Palazzo di Montecitorio (17th century)

Piazza Montecitorio, 33

Pope Innocent X commissioned Gian Lorenzo Bernini to plan the building. Bernini started the work in 1650, for his nephew Nicolo Ludovisi. It is said that Bernini won the contract after having shown the Prince and his wife a model of the *palazzo* made in silver. In 1654, the year that Ludovisi died, the work was halted due to insufficient funds. It picked up again only when the *palazzo* had been bought by Pope Innocent XII, who assigned Carlo Fontana to complete the *palazzo* (1677), transforming it into the Court House.

The façade is based on floors that are oblique and receding and that suggest a diminishing perspective, breaking with the orthogonal outline and plan, which was common at that time. Ashlar work that hinge onto the ground floor and that sustain the gigantic order of the upper floors with irregular rocks, is a mimicry of architecture, typical of the Baroque. The foundation with its receding sides, is to be attributed to Bernini, while the architectural solutions of the central part of the building are of Fontana. This with the few variants that of the simplification of the windows, the door with three horizontally developed axes, and the whole pointed motive in the central part, manage to transform the character of the *palazzo* that gives a sense of gentleness to a public office.

The halls of the *palazzo* are enriched by many paintings by artists such as Guercino, Luca Giordano and Paolo Veronese. There is also an archeological collection that comes from the Vulci necropolis, which is conserved in the *palazzo*.

In 1902 Ernesto Basile presented a project to enlarge the *palazzo* which included the use of the Art Deco style for the back façade.

In 1870 the building was chosen as the seat for the Chamber of Deputies.

[AF]

37 – Palazzo Nuovo in Campidoglio (17th century)
Piazza del Campidoglio

The *palazzo* is of the same form as Palazzo dei Conservatori, which was part of the general project to organize Piazza del Campidoglio by Michelangelo, that has a wing perspective of the piazza.

The foundations had been laid in the time of Clement VIII (1603), but the work was done under Innocent X by Girolamo and Carlo Rainaldi. For the longest time an unfinished wall, instead of the *palazzo*, was the only thing that stood and sustained a fountain by Giacomo Della Porta, decorated by the fluvial statue said to be by Marforio. The same statue can now be seen in the courtyard, and it has been there since 1679. It represents the Ocean and it is one of the four "statue parlante" – speaking statues – of Rome, the others being Pasquino, dell'Abate Luigi and Madama Lucrezia.

On the first floor of the *palazzo*, there is a scanned façade of eight pilaster strips which each end with a capital in Corithian style, on which there is a large frame overhung by a balustrade with statues on it. The pilaster strips frame the seven windows of which the centre one is triangularly arched and the other is gabled at the center. On the ground floor, there is a large doorway that leads into the *palazzo*.

The *palazzo* was used as a depository for the art of the building and was then given over to the University of Art and Trade and only in 1734 was it finally assigned to the museum. [AF]

38 – Palazzo Pecci Blunt (16th century)
Via dell'Ara Coeli, 3

This *palazzo*, with its simple and elegant façade facing the Michelangelo stairway in the Campidoglio, was built in the first half of the sixteenth century for the Albertoni family, unrivaled rulers of this quarter. Of ancient Roman origin, the family was well known for their venerated ancestor Ludovica, immortalized in Bernini's sculpture *Blessed Ludovica Albertoni*, for the Church of San Francesco at Ripa. Cardinals and administrators, the Paluzzi Albertoni lived in their quarter, building other homes on the Campitelli and Margana piazzas.

Around 1550, the *palazzo* on Piazza dell'Aracoeli was acquired by Cardinal Silvestro Gottardi. Soon after, it was bought by Maria Fani; the Fani family had the *palazzo* restructured by Giacomo della Porta (1532–1602), who later bought an adjacent building. Several decades later the *palazzo* passed to the Marchese Bartolomeo Ruspoli, who lived there before moving to his home on the Via del Corso. Early in the seventeenth

century the building became the home of the Malatesta counts, and in 1929 it became the property of the Pecci Blunt family, its current owners.

The *palazzo* originally had two floors topped by an elegant cornice; the linear architraves of the windows on the second floor repeat the motif of the main door. A roof terrace added during the nineteenth century gives the *palazzo* a panoramic view. Rusticated stonework runs along the entire length of the building on the outside corners. The jewel of this construction was the stuccoed loggia with its wealth of frescoes and gilding. Students of the Zuccaro brothers worked in the vast apartments of the *piano nobile*, including Ventura Salimbeni and Gaspard Dughet. Ventura Salimbeni was probably the primary artist of one cycle of frescoes.

The frescoes by Federico and Taddeo Zuccaro and their assistants reflect the dictates of the Manneristic style. The Sala degli Arazzi still has original Flemish tapestries. From the entry one passes through a small private chapel. On the walls are four paintings of the evangelists by Lucas van Leyden.

The Pecci Blunt family, current owners of the *palazzo*, have restored the gallery on the ground floor using marbles from the famous Medici company, the same company that earlier restored the *piano nobile*. [CVM]

39 – Palazzo Pamphili (18th century)
Piazza Navona, 14

The Pamphili family were gentry from Gubbio since 1150. They moved to Rome in the 1400s where they began buying numerous buildings apart from Piazza Novana and Piazza Pasquino. Their greatness was achieved when Giovan Battista Pamphili was elected Pope with the name of Innocent X (1644-1655). Pope Innocent united all the property commissioning Girolamo Rainaldi into an imposing building. The *palazzo* became the "royal *palazzo* " of Lady Olimpia Maidalchini, widow of Innocent's brother Pamphilio Pamphili. Olimpia was a very ambitious and greedy woman, and she became the most influential figure in the Papal Court. She was a true "Popess" and her reputation was so universally bad that she was nicknamed "la Pimpaccia" di Piazza Navona and "Olym pia" which is Latin means "once virtuous".

The construction of the *palazzo* went on between 1644 and 1650, and developed horizontally. It had two façades on Piazza Navona and the other on Via di Santa Maria dell' Anima. The façade facing the piazza seems to thicken the significant architectural elements around the central balcony, which is supported by four columns taken from the St Peter's Basilica. The two upper floors have windows with acute gables or semilunar gables inserted in blind arches, with the Pamphili family shield dominating in the center. Apart from the crowning cornice you can find an imposing loggia of five arches flanked by a 19th century rising terrace.

Inside, the *palazzo* is rich with painted decorations and beautiful stuccos. There is also the famous gallery of Pietro da Corton, on the immense vault there are scenes from the life of Aeneas and it is illuminated by the Serliana, whereby one can see the architectural style of Borromini.

In1960 the *palazzo* became the seat of the Brazilian Embassy. [AF]

40 – Casino di Pio IV (16th century)
Giardini Vaticani

Between 1559 and 1562, Pirro Ligorio built this cottage in the Vatican gardens, in the most elaborately antiquated way possible. This Mannerist vision dominates the rediscovered purist form of Renaissance style.
The building that connects the lodge and a smaller one-floor building with an elliptic courtyard is a typical example of the beautiful cottages of the villas of the late Renaissance period. The external decorations are by Rocco da Motefiascone, while the internal frescoes are by Federico Zuccari and Barocci.
Pius XI had the cottage enlarged by adding a new wing and restored the Pontificia Accademia delle Scienze – The Papal Academy of Science – in 1936. [AF]

41 – Palazzo del Quirinale (16th century)
Piazza del Quirinale

Casting about for somewhere that might offer him relief from the oppressive heat of the Roman summer, Pope Gregory XIII (1572–85) asked his friend Ippolito d'Este for his land up on the Quirinal, the highest of Rome's seven hills. Ippolito gave it to him willingly since he himself was directing all his energies southward, to Tivoli.

During the so-called Babylonian captivity (1309–78) the popes had lived in Avignon. The decision was finally made to build a new residence on the top of the Quirinal Hill in the area that was known as Monte Cavallo because of the two sculptural groups of the Dioscuri with their horses that had been found there. That residence, today known as the Quirinal, has been a close participant in the history of Rome and the Italian nation, for the Renaissance *palazzo* has gone from being the summer home of the popes to being the primary residence of the kings of Italy to being the home of Italy's president.

The most celebrated artists of each period have been called upon to work on the *palazzo*, and each has done so using, of course, his period's prevailing style. The industrious Gregory XIII began the process by calling on Ottaviano Mascherino to build the first *palazzo*. The structure Mascherino built between 1583 and 1585 today constitutes the left wing of the *palazzo*, with the façade with loggia that forms one of the shorter side fronts giving onto the grand courtyard. Mascherino also designed the magnificent oval spiral staircase with coupled columns that connects the first and second floors.

No sooner had Gregory XIII begun this work than he died; he was succeeded by one of the most extraordinary characters in papal history, Sixtus V (1585–90). Sixtus V had only five years as pope, but in that short time he managed to revolutionize the appearance of the city. His chief architect was Domenico Fontana, responsible for the initial arrangement of the Piazza of the Quirinal with the statuary group of the two Dioscuri that had once embellished the baths of Constantine. Fontana began work on the new *palazzo* on Monte Cavallo that faced onto the piazza. At this time the small building made by Mascherino was connected to the new

palazzo by way of a long, low structure that was used at first to house the Swiss Guards but was destined for further changes under the pontificate of Paul V. Sixtus V was followed by a series of lesser popes who did little to the city and the Quirinal except carry on or complete works already in progress. No sooner had Paul V (1605-21) been made pope than he decided to finally finish the building, commissioning Flaminio Ponzio to integrate the structures made by Mascherino and Fontana, to build the datary (the office in charge of registering and dating bulls, overseeing the payment of duties, and other official tasks), and to ready a new series of rooms for decoration. At Ponzio's death in 1613, Carlo Maderno was put in charge of the worksite, and he contributed to several projects, including the planning of the two large sides, extending the building along the road that at that time led to Porta Pia. He finished the pretty rectangular courtyard and designed the chapel of the Annunciation, frescoed

Agostino Tassi, *The Ambassadors* (1616)

by Guido Reni, for the private devotions of his patron. Maderno also built the elaborate portal communicating between the chapel and the Sala Regia, topped by two angels by Pietro Bernini and a high-relief by Taddeo Landini, showing *Christ Washing the Feet of the Disciples*.

Whereas Paul V made the Quirinal into a sort of second Vatican, Urban VIII (1623–44) wanted to turn it into a fortress. To render the *palazzo* nothing less than impregnable, he had it surrounded by ramparts and high walls. Gian Lorenzo Bernini, official architect of the pope and his family, designed the benediction loggia above the portal, where Urban appeared to dispense blessings.

Work began again under Alexander VII (1655–57), during whose short papacy the arts experienced an exceptional flourishing. A learned man, dignified and polite, he commissioned an astonishing number of renovations. The leader in this was Bernini, who planned a new series of halls for the Quirinal. It was during these years that the structure housing the Swiss Guards was remodeled and raised one floor higher. During the eighteenth century the obelisk was set in place above the fountain, and Innocent XIII (1721–24) commissioned Alessandro Specchi to design the stables. Clement XII (1730–40) retired to the Quirinal immediately after his coronation as pope and commissioned Ferdinando Fuga (1699–1782) to build the "long wing" of the *palazzo* of the Consulta that faces the Quirinal, and had the famous Palazzina built on the site of several modest little houses and a corner of the garden. Benedict XIV (1740–58) also asked Fuga to design a coffee house, as such structures were known.

Napoleon was scheduled to visit in 1812, and the preparations for this event involved further reworking of the halls of the Quirinal Palazzo. Imperial apartments were readied, and a team of neoclassical artists was assembled. The French emperor never made the visit, but the rooms made ready are still intact, as are the fiery decorations made by Giani.

Having served as the official summer residence of the popes from 1592 on, the Quirinal Palace began a new chapter with the decline in ecclesiastical pomp that began in 1870 with the birth of the Kingdom of Italy. New ballrooms, many of them reflecting questionable nineteenth-century taste, were built, often replacing antique decorations. Since 1947 the *palazzo* has been the residence of the president of the Italian republic. [CVM]

42 – Palazzo Rondinini (18th century)
Via del Corso, 318

The spirit of classical antiquity once pervaded this *palazzo* to an almost obsessive degree, testimony to the devotion for things Greco-Roman that gripped wealthy collectors during the eighteenth century. Ever since the Renaissance, architects in Rome were called upon to design buildings for art collectors, and this *palazzo* on Via Lata came into being primarily to house such a collection, that of Giuseppe Rondinini. The architect Alessandro Dori kept his client's archaeological obsession very much in mind and used the marquis's taste and erudition in the design of his home, the architecture of which harmoniously blends carved marbles and marble fragments, inscriptions and columns of gray granite, slabs of ancient yel-

low porphyry and black African porphyry. The building dates back to a small *palazzo* near the Piazza del Popolo that Margherita Ambra Rondinini, Giuseppe's mother, had bought in 1744.

Giuseppe Cesari (1568–1640) had made this building to serve as his own family residence. His social standing and the artistic fame he had achieved during the pontificate of Clement VIII allowed him, in 1604, to buy for 3,000 scudi an unfinished *palazzo* on the Via del Corso. The last member of the Cesari family, Giuseppe dei Cesari di Arpino, left the *palazzo* to the Barnabite fathers, who sold it shortly afterward to Giuseppe's mother. Nothing remains of this first structure except mentions in chronicles that describe its size. Originally from Romagna, the Rondinini family had moved to Rome in 1572 to begin a glorious social ascent. By carefully managing his capital, Giuseppe Rondinini was able to avoid the reversals that impoverished the great majority of Rome's aristocracy. During the second half of the eighteenth century he had the *palazzo* restored and organized a magnificent collection of paintings. Remodeled and enlarged by Alessandro Dori, the *palazzo* in Via del Corso was completely transformed. The body of the building, which extended toward the Church of San Giacomo, was enlarged. In keeping with the new style, according to which the monumental and vast halls of the baroque were to be replaced with smaller, more comfortable rooms, Dori designed highly accessible rooms softened by a new sense of intimacy.

The Capranica family inherited the *palazzo*, which then passed to the banker Feoli. The building was rented to the Russian embassy during the nineteenth century, and an Orthodox chapel was built that has since disappeared. Since 1946, the owner of the *palazzo* has been the Banca Nazionale dell'Agricoltura, which bought it from the last heir of the Sanseverino. The new owners have brought an end to the destruction of the building caused by arbitrary alterations and the scattering of its belongings. [CVM]

43 – Palazzo Ruspoli Rucellai
Largo Goldoni, 56

This enormous structure with its severe features faces Via del Corso, once known as Via Lata, the main avenue that had been the center of the city since the seventeenth century, thus enjoying the role that had belonged in antiquity to the Campus Martius when the emperor Augustus had decided to build his mausoleum on that site. Many Roman families had built their *palazzos* along this avenue, amid the remains of the Ara Pacis (Altar of Peace) and the Arco di Portogallo (demolished during the reign of Pope Alexander VII). During the Carnival celebrations on the eve of Lent the balconies and façades of buildings along the avenue were elaborately decorated. An early structure had been built by the family of the Jacobilli, who had moved to Rome from Foligno to carry on their careers as city administrators. Little remains of that ancient structure, however, for it was entirely reworked in 1583, on the initiative of Orazio Rucellai, by Bartlomeo Ammanati.

With Orazio's death, in 1605, the splendid *palazzo* became the property of his sons Luigi and then Ferdinando. Since Ferdinando was without heirs, he transferred it to Luigi Caetani, in 1629, for the price of 51,000 florins. Under the guidance of Bartolomeo Breccioli, a family architect, extensive renovations were undertaken. Breccioli directed various improvements in the cornice and the mezzanines, designing the façade on Via dei Fontanella Boghese. The cardinal had Martino Longhi II erect a staircase entirely covered with slabs of Parian marble. Statues were set in niches. The Caetani family's heavy debts, combined with the gradual erosion of their political influence, must certainly have influenced their decision to sell the property, in 1713, to the Ruspoli family.

Francesco Maria Marescotti Ruspoli brought a lively and extroverted spirit to the salons, which proved well suited to the new life being led there. Theatrical performances were held in the Salone delle Accademia similar to those that Cardinal Pietro Ottoboni arranged in the Cancelleria, but it was music more than anything else that reached levels of exquisite quality under the prince's guidance. Austerity having fallen out of fashion, the rooms on the ground floor were decorated with an extraordinary variety of col-

orful decorative cycles. Views of the family's estates were followed by playful works by Antonio Amorosi, who painted scenes of popular celebrations during country outings, at which times the villas were thrown open to peasants. Many of the famous guests who stayed in the rooms of Palazzo Ruspoli, from the duke of Nevers to Cardinal Borgia, whiled away time trying to decipher the mysterious harmony of the gallery's painted vault. In 1830, the *palazzo* was visited by the former queen of Holland Hortense de Beauharnais, who arrived with her son, the future Napoleon III. [CVM]

The gallery decorated by Jacopo Zucchi >

44 – Palazzo Sacchetti (16th century)
Via Giulia, 66

For almost twenty years, Antonio da Sangallo the Younger (1484–1546) reigned uncontested in Rome as the favorite architect of the rising aristocracy. He designed Palazzo Sacchetti in Via Giulia for himself and his family but he died in 1546, work on the *palazzo* had only just begun.

The new owner was Cardinal Giovanni Ricci of Montepulciano, who bought the *palazzo* in 1552. New rooms were planned following the acquisition of the adjacent house owned by the Massari brothers of Narni.

In 1553, when the work was completed, Francesco Salviati was called to fresco the central hall, known as the Salone del Mappamondo. With the cardinal's death in 1576, ownership of the *palazzo* passed to the Ceuli, a family of Pisan bankers who had moved to Rome. They saw to the completion of its decoration and used it to house a collection of antique sculpture. The layout of the building was considerably altered with the addition of two new wings and a loggia facing the river and overlooking the garden.

In 1608 the *palazzo* became the property of Cardinal Ottavio Aquaviva of Aragon, who had a private chapel built.

Since 1649 the *palazzo* has been home to the Sacchetti family, who moved from Fiesole, above Florence. Under these new owners the *palazzo* experienced a true rebirth. Their home became a center of refined patronage as the two Sacchetti brothers carefully created a splendid picture collection. The dome and the lantern at the center of the private chapel were certainly conceived early in Pietro da Cortona's career and were decorated by Agostino Ciampelli. In the dining room overlooking the Tiber, in the wing that had been built by the banker Ceuli, he made two frescoes, Adam and Eve and The Holy Family. In 1660, Carlo Rainaldi was called in to change the grotto, which he had flanked by a wall along the Tiber side where people could play boccie. The loggias were closed in halfway through the nineteenth century, but the part of the building overlooking the river, built on a design by Giovan Battista Contini, has been standing since 1699.
[CVM]

45 – Palazzo San Callisto (sec.xvi-xviii)
Piazza di Santa Maria in Trastevere, 24

The *palazzo* was built in the 1400s by order of the Cardinal – owner of the church of Santa Maria in Trastevere, who also had custody of a small church called San Callisto. According to legend, it appears that the building was constructed on a Roman house where Pope Callistus I was taken by surprise while praying, by some Roman pagans on the rampage for Christians in the Settimio Severo era. The *palazzo* has been restored many times. In 1434 Eugene IV restored it. In 1505 Cardinalo Vigerio di Savon had it restored and enlarged to its current form, by Orazio Torrigiani to compensate the Benedettinis because their head office had been demolished in order to make room for Palazzo del Quirinale. The last time it was restored was in 1854 by Pope Pius XI. The façade that looks onto the piazza is in front of a large fountain by Carlo Fontana. The façade is composed of two series of architraved ashlar worked windows. The main door is softened at the keystone by a caryatid which contributes to supporting the balcony. At the center of the upper floor there is central window with a spaced out centered gable. Here you can find the shield pertaining to Pius XI in marble, and a zigzag cornice that crowns the building.

After 1870 the *palazzo* was taken over by the Italian State and used as a barracks; only in 1907 was it given back to the Holy See. [AF]

46 – Palazzo Santacroce (15th-16th centuries)
Via in Publicolis, 43

The Santacroce family boasted that they were the descendents of the Roman Consul Publius Valerius Publicola, and have been present in Rome since the XII century.

They say that for the "tracontanza o turbolenza" – arrogance or unruliness, by many members of the family, Sextus IV (1412 –1484) apparently had their houses demolished so that they would leave the city. In any case between the 1500s and the 1600s the Santacroce family had four Cardinals. It was thanks to Cardinal Prospero Santacroce that at the time of Pope Pius IV (1559-1565) that tobacco was introduced to Rome and it was initially called "erba Santacroce" – "Santacroce weed".

After 1484, Antonio Santacrose had the *palazzo* built in its present form: three floors with angular towers striped in ashlar work with a diamond point and travertine covered façades. The first two floors have architraved windows with a simple show and the third, raised non-architraved windows in the 1600's style. Certain decorative characteristics seem to be originally Catalonian, considering their similarity to the house of Pico of the 15th century in Segovia in Spain. [AF]

47 – Palazzo Savelli Orsini (16th century)
Via Monte Savello, 30

The theater of Marcellus stood at the heart of the ancient city, in the monumental zone where enormous buildings crowded side by side along the city blocks, forming a towering spectacle that must have astonished and stupefied the foreigners who made their way into the great Urbs by one of its sixteen gates. During the Middle Ages the area around the theater was the most densely populated of the city. Since it dominated the three bridges that joined the city to the Tiber Island and thus to Trastevere it was of strategic importance. During the thirteenth century the building was included in the property of the aristocratic Fabii family, as indicated by the ancient name Monte Fabiorum, although the Pierleoni are later cited as the principal owners. A century later, in 1361, the theater is listed among the properties of the Savelli family, who early on built a fortified *palazzo* on that spot from which to dominate their holdings. An interesting document dated February 24, 1279, includes the will of Cardinal Giacomo Savelli, who names as his heirs Leone and Giovanni, confirming that the building belonged to the Savelli family on that date. The power of the medieval noble houses began to wane, but the Savelli house maintained much of its power and glory until the sixteenth century. In 1535 they had a new *palazzo* built atop the ancient fortifications, and as architect they chose Baldassare Peruzzi (1481–1536), who was in Rome that year for the last time in his life. Above the ancient theater he built a two-story structure composed of three rectangular wings facing a central courtyard, an arrangement that is no longer visible because it was thoroughly altered by nineteenth-century renovations. The main entrance opened in a high wall with battlements that served to protect the building from flooding of the Tiber.

When the last heir of the ancient Savelli family died in 1712, the *palazzo* came into the possession of the Sforza Cesarini. It then became the property of Domenico Orsini, prince of Gravina. During the eighteenth century minor artists decorated the piano nobile and nineteenth-century architects thoroughly erased what remained of the architectural elements designed by Peruzzi, reworking the areas created by that great Sienese artist.

Ancient records indicate that the Savelli family itself rented out the ground floor to butchers and artisans from the thirteenth century onward, and chronicles from 1920 speak of little shops doing a lively business under the ancient arches. [CVM]

Matteo Pacini, *Crowning of the Virgin* (1370)

48 – Palazzo Senatorio (16th century)
Piazza Del Campidoglio, 1

Palazzo Senatorio rests on an area which is predominantly occupied by tabularium. It is the seat of the Public Archive of Rome, going back to 78 B.C. It was positioned to respect the ruins of the Vejove temple. Vejove was an Etruscan divinity. In the 12th century the *palazzo* was built, fortified by the community, on the same land as the tabularium.

In 1536, when Emperor Charles V visited Rome, Pope Paul II, embarrassed by the state the Campidoglio was in, asked Michelangelo Buonarroti to come up with a project that would renew the piazza and the façade of the Palazzo dei Conservatori and Palazzo Senatorio. The work started in 1546 but Michelangelo managed to supervise only on the double staircase of entry to the *palazzo*. Giacomo Della Porta and Girolamo Rainaldi did the rest. They did nothing other than recover the antique mediaeval building with simple plaster. Two lateral foreparts, the angular towers built in the 13 and 1400s by Popes Boniface IX, Martion V and Nicholas V, give movement to the façade. The façade is scaled by Corinthian parastades that separate the alternated curved and triangular gabled windows that are surmounted by small-halved windows. On the prospect, where Michelangelo would have wanted a majestic Capitolian Jove, there is a small seated statue that comes from the temple of Cori, and a restorer has transformed it into the divinity of Rome. The tower with its squared section by Martino Longhi the Elder, with his motive of large arches between the twin column parastades, is divided in half by the center clock and it is decorated by the coat-of-arms and heraldic elements.

The *palazzo* is called Senatorio – Of the Senate – because up until 1870 it was the residence of the Senator of Rome. Today it is the seat of Town Hall offices of Rome. [AF]

49 – Palazzetti settecenteschi (18th century)

Piazza Sant'Ignazio

In 1725 Pope Benedict XIII insisted that the Jesuits finally fix the space facing Sant'Ignazio church, which had been built by Alessandro Algardi (mid 17th century). The Jesuits commissioned Filippo Raguzzini who completed the work in only three years, from 1727 to 1730. He repeated the traditional way of the masters of the 17th century who preferred a closed piazza similar to a court, rather than one with a vast view. Raguzzin proposed an intimate piazza, where the simple house, and not the façades of the churches, became the central focal point. This activated one of the most characteristic urban arrangements of the 1700s. The elegance of the curvilinear design comes about by following the tangential point of three ovals: the biggest one determines the bending of the central *palazzo* and the two lateral ones influences the edges of this *palazzo*, and those edges of the two *palazzos* that close the sides on the piazza. The façades of the buildings with three floors, which are limited by large cornices, have been built with recovered brick from the ruins of Roman forums and today they are plastered. They are characteristic of the great chamfers that close in the window by a decorated colonnade.

In 1792, during the brief Roman Jacobean Republic, the France Administration used the *palazzo* for its offices. [AF]

50 – Palazzo Spada
Piazza di Capo di Ferro, 13

At the height of their power and fortune, the Capodiferro family commissioned the architect Bartolomeo Baronino to build an elegant residence for Cardinal Girolamo. Work began in 1549 and kept to such a brisk pace that the *palazzo* had been completed by the spring of 1550. The façade of the *palazzo* dates to that period and is still intact. Its decorations in stucco, fresco, and graffito work follow a style that was widespread in the first half of the sixteenth century and that had conferred on the city a sense of gaiety and artistic complexity that is now difficult to imagine. Standing over the main door is the coat-of-arms of the building's patron, Paul III, whose grandiose *palazzo* had recently been built nearby with the assistance of Baronino. The courtyard and the façade were both decorated by Giulio Mazzoni, and both have niches holding antique-style

figures of Olympian divinities alternating with the coats-of-arms of Julius II and Henry II of France. Inside the *palazzo*, the series of rooms on the *piano nobile* constitutes an impressive repertory of Manneristic style. In 1632, the *palazzo* was bought by Cardinal Bernardino Spada and his brother Virgilio, and under their ownership it experienced a rebirth during the baroque period. Bernardino began directing the restoration and expansion of the building, adding another wing. Borromini designed the famous example of trompe l'oeil for Palazzo Spada. This magnificent arched colonnade is only thirty feet long but seems far longer, its columns rapidly diminishing as they recede from the viewer: what seems to be a life-size statue at the end is, in reality, barely a foot tall. He displayed a similar curious bent when he made the gallery with the solar and lunar sundial. During his time in Bologna, Bernardino Spada had come into contact with the two leading perspective painters of the time, Angelo Michele Colonna

(1604–1687) and Agostino Mitelli (1609–1660). He summoned both these artists to Rome to make the ornamental decoration of the so-called Sala di Pompeo.

Now owned by the Italian state, Palazzo Spada is headquarters of the Council of State. The arched colonnade by Borromini is open to the public, as is the seventeenth-century gallery, which houses Bernardino's collection of paintings and sculpture in a suitably baroque atmosphere. [CVM]

Giulio Mazzoni, The Stucco Gallery

The statue of Pompeo in the Pompeo Room >

51 – Palazzo Taverna Gabrielli Orsini (from 13th century)

Via Monte Giordano, 36

The ancient fortress of the Orsini family was built on the hill known as Monte Giordano. During its earliest stages this citadel was much like a small, independent town, with its own central piazza surrounded by palaces and its own church, the whole assembly defended by towers with battlements at every corner.

A document dated October 21, 1286, indicates that three brothers of Pope Nicholas III were living on the hill at that time. Before this, the hill had been inhabited by the ancient and noble families of the Boveschi and the Stefaneschi; it was named Monte Giordano after Giordano di Poncello, a courageous follower of the revolutionary Cola di Rienzo (who was killed in 1354). Midway through the sixteenth century Cardinal Ippolito d'Este, life tenant of Prince Camillo, made the *palazzo* the site of a splendid court, alternating his stays in Rome with rest periods in the Villa of Tivoli. The exterior of the *palazzo* still has the spare and severe Renaissance architectural elements it had under the Orsini. Also dating from that period is the portico, although it has lost the beautiful stairway. However, in 1688 the house on Monte Giordano was sold by court order, and ownership passed to the Gabrielli family.

Prince Pietro Gabrielli did nothing to change the exterior's Renaissance simplicity, turning his attention instead to the interior rooms, which he had transformed into luxurious halls. The prince had the interior apartments redecorated and frescoed on the occasion of the marriage, in 1815, of his son Mario to Charlotte Bonaparte. From 1809 to his death in 1816, Coccetti worked alone, a rare instance of individual effort in a period when such decorations were carried out by entire teams of artists. Although locked away in his gilt prison, Coccetti somehow intuited the classical-revival style of the Directoire period, creating works that can be set alongside the mythologies of David and the billowy landscapes of Fragonard.

The Gabrielli family collected precious tapestries and a magnificent series of paintings by Sebastiano Ricci (1659–1734) and Giovanni Battista Pittoni (1687–1767). Built during the heyday of the gens Orsina, the monumental fountain with two pools splashing with water from the Acqua

Paola aqueduct was restored in the eighteenth century by Antonio Casoni. Unwise speculations in the building industry led to the sudden collapse of the Gabrielli fortune, forcing the family to transfer ownership of the *palazzo* on Monte Giordano in 1888. The Milanese family of the Taverna counts, relatives of the current owners, acquired the group of buildings. Even today, in part because of their undecorated walls and in part because of the remnants of ancient towers, these buildings have something of the severe sense of a fortress. [CVM]

52 – Palazzo Torlonia Giraud (16th century)
Via della Conciliazione, 130

It was built at the end of the 1400s for Cardinal Castellesi da Corneto, Secretary to Alexander VI. It was later donated in 1505 to the King of England who assigned to have the English Embassy there, in the Papal State. The Giraud family subsequently bought the *palazzo*. They were a French banking family and in the 1600s they gave it up to the Torlonia family, also bankers, who restored and extended it.

The façade, a fine example of the Renaissance era, can be attributed – according to Vasari – to Bramante, though critics say it is probable that it could be attributed to Andrea Bregno. The façade is divided into three series of two string-course strips, where seven windows are scanned by pilaster strips. The windows of the first floor are centered and architraved, while on the second floor they are rectangular with smaller windows overhead. You can just make out the courtyard, attributed to Raffaello, adorned by statues and two fountains just across from the arched doorway bearing the Torlonia coat-of-arms. [AF]

53 – Palazzetto Casina Valadier (19th century)

Via Del Belvedere al Pincio

Palazzetto Casina Valadier is named after the architect Giuseppe Valadier, commissioned by Cardinal Della Porta, who transformed it from a country cottage into a small *palazzo* in perfect neoclassic form. It took Valadier five years to accomplish this, from 1813 to 1817.

Various activities occurred at the cottage, some less fortuitous than others, even though, at one point it was *the* place to be seen. In 1816 Antonio Antonini opened the cottage up to the public and it was frequented by the intellectuals of the time. In 1870 it was taken over by the Town Hall of Rome, and in 1922 it was changed into a café and remembered in daily life during the years between the two wars.

The building was constructed over a Roman water cistern. The cistern had been built to water the Aciliani crops that ran along the Pincio River. People would hide in the underground pipes and used them to escape during the pillage of Rome in 1527.

The cottage, modified in a definitively 14th century manner, presents a colonnade ending in a vault built in 1922. At the same time the belvedere terrace was extended and provides an incomparable view the city.

Near the balustrade there is a bust of the astrologer Secchi. At its base there is a small hole which indicates the point where the meridian of Rome passes.

[AF]

54 – Palazzo Valentini (end 16th century)
Via Cesare Battisti, 119

The *palazzo* was Emperor Hadrian's temple. He dedicated it to the memory of Trajan, and Cardinal Michele Bonelli commissioned it to Friar Domenico Paganelli da Faenza near the end of the 16th century.

In the first half of the 1600s, it became the property of the Imperial Cardinal, and was demolished and the restructured based on a project by Francesco Paparelli. At the end of the 1700s the banker Vincenzo Valentini bought it.

The Valentini family, rich owners of an important export company from Civitavecchia, opened a bank in Rome with the help of the architect Filippo Navone. Between them, they made the *palazzo* so luxurious that it was in competition with the *palazzos* of the Colonna the Torlonia families. At the same time it became a meeting place for people of learning in the 1700s.

The building is a pure rectangular volume defined by cantonal ashlar work the runs the whole height. The main façade of the building is scanned by three different fascias with different designs. On the ground floor there is a large doorway with two Ionic columns, overhanging with an ample balcony on to which the window of the first floor opens. Harmonious lines emerge from the vestibule which takes you to the courtyard. On the top floors the seven windows per floor are alternately triangularly architraved highly centered windows. On the second floor the windows are simply framed. There is a crowned cornice supported by three-tiered brackets with smaller windows inserted alternately.

The halls are frescoed beautifully and there are paintings from the school of Caravaggio and famous statues like that of Aphrodite, Valentini, Apollo, Pizio and Athens. [AF]

55 – Palazzo Venezia (15th century)
Piazza Venezia, 3

Built by the Venetian Cardinal Pietro Barbo, who transferred to Rome in 1440. He was later appointed Pontiff in 1464 with the name of Paul II (1464-14710. Palazzo Venezia is the first grand Roman *palazzo* in the modern and Renaissance sense while still maintaining some characteristics of sobriety like the crenelation façade with cruciform windows and a "cardinalizia" tower. Francesco del Borgo, the humanist architect who projected it, created a spiritual masterpiece of the Renaissance period. Still showing signs of ties with tradition, the magnificence of the halls in their decorative architectural elements, such as the incomplete central courtyard and the loggia in front of the Church of San Marco together form a base for the evolution of Roman Renaissance.

The vicissitude of the *palazzo* illuminates the irregular aspects of the building. Pietro Barbo became Cardinal of the church of San Marco in 1451. He decided to restructure the *palazzo* between 1454 and 1455. This was done a little before the Papal election in 1464. This first *palazzo* comprised only of the façade that is actually on Piazza Venezia, and that goes as far as the main door (by Giovanni Dalmata) and it was lower and without a courtyard. After the Papal election the pontiff decided to transform it into a grandiose residence. The work began in 1468 and continued after his death, by order of Cardinal Lorenzo Cybo for a further 20 years. In 1471 the work got as far as the doorway on Via del Plesbiscito.

Apart from representing the Cardinal's residence at San Marco, Palazzo Venezia also represented the seat of the Pontiffs who could not yet use the building in the hills of Quirinale, as it was still under construction.

The last Pontiff to hold residence there was Clement VIII (1592-1605). In the 1600s a lot of work was done in order to embellish the *palazzo* with constant beauty. Both the Cardinals of San Marco and the Venetian Ambassadors of the time who also made use of part of the *palazzo* contributed to the *palazzo* artistically.

Internally there are numerous works of art. The "Mappamondo" hall is decorated by Andrea Mantegna and the "Regia" hall has traces of paintings by Bramante in it. With the agreement of Campoformio in 1797 Palazzo

Venezia was haunded over to Napoleon's France and then in 1814 to Austria.

In 1908 with the construction of the monument dedicated to Victor Emanuel II, the debate about the surrounding area started up again. In order to regulate Piazza Venezia it was decided to demolish and reconstruct the palezzetto Venezia. This meant reducing the arcade on the side of the courtyard and restricting the surrounding area. Even the small church of Madonna della Grazie was reconstructed between via del Plesbiscito and Piazza Venezia.

At the beginning of the First World War, the whole complex was confiscated by the Italian State; then between 1924 and 1930 it was restored. During the twenty years of fascism it was used as the seat of the Government and the Fascist Committee. Benito Mussolini used it as his war headquarters, stirring up the crowds from the main balcony.

It is now the seat of the permanent Museum and the Library of History of Art. [AF]

56 – Palazzo Zuccari (16th-17th centuries)
Piazza Trinita dei Monti, 14

The Mannerist painter Federico Zuccari, scholar and then collaborator with his brother Taddeo, projected in 1592 a complex use of Palazzo Zuccari. It was to be used as a residence and a studio, to be built between Via Gregoriana and Via Sistina. On his tombstone it read "Federico Zuccari the Academy of Art and Design is your home and residence for you and yours, he built this house and his painting adorn it".

The building is astonishing for its originality of decoration on the doors and on the windows, and on the façade overlooking Via Gregoriana. Zuccari modelled a lot of his work on the famous park of Villa Orsini a Bomarzo, near Viterbo.

In the course of the years the *palazzo* changed its aspect and its owners. In 1609 it was sold to Matteo Toscanelli who assigned Girolamo Rainaldi between 1610 and 1618 to modernize the part of the building that looked towards Trinità dei Monti. In 1702 the Queen Maria Casimira of Poland rented it and had Filippo Juvara make a little portico with a Tuscan colonnade. When Alessandro Nazzari took over the building he turned it in to a famous lodge, a meeting place for foreign artists when in Rome.

In 1904, Enrichetta Hertz created an impressive library and left that and the *palazzo* to the German Government. Today it houses the Hertzian Library that specializes in Art History in Medieaval and Modern Art. The *palazzo* has become famous because Gabriele D'Annunzio's protagonist imagines the residence in his book *Il piacere*. [AF]

Bibliography

AMAYDEN, T., *Storia delle famiglie romane*, Rome, no date.

AMMANNATO, C., *Via Giulia*, Rome 1989.

ASHBY, T., "The Palazzo Odescalchi in Rome", *Papers of the British School of Rome*, VIII, 1916 and 1920.

BORSI, F., *Palazzo Rondinini*, Rome 1983.

– *Palazzo del Quirinale*, Rome 1991.

BENZI, F., *Sisto IV Renovator Urbis. Architettura a Roma 1471-1484*, Rome 1990.

BRIGANTI, G., *Palazzo del Quirinale*, Rome 1962.

BRUSCHI, A., *Bramante architetto*, Bari 1969.

CÀLLARI, L., *Le ville di Roma*, Rome 1934.

– *I PALAZZI di Roma*, Rome 1944.

CANNATÀ, R., *Guida a Palazzo Spada*, Rome 1984.

CARANDENTE, G., *Il palazzo Doria Pamphili*, Milan 1975.

CHASTEL, A. and MOREL, P., *La villa Médicis. Académie de France à Rome*, Rome 1989.

COARELLI, F., *Guida archeologica di Roma*, Milan 1974.

COFFIN, D.R., *The Villa in the Life of Renaissance Rome*, Princeton 1979.

– *GARDENS and Gardening in Papal Rome*, Princeton 1991.

DE FEO, V., *La piazza del Quirinale. Storia, architettura e urbnistica*, Rome, 1973.

DELLA PERGOLA, P., *Villa Borghese*, Rome 1962.

FAGIOLO DELL'ARCO, M., *Bernini*, Rome 1967.

FERRERIO, P., *Palazzi di Roma de' più celebri architetti*, Rome 1650.

FROMMEL, C.L., *Baldassare Peruzzi als maler und Zeichner*, Vienna 1967-68.

– *DER RÖMISCHE Palastbau der Hocherenaissance*, I, Tubingen 1973.

– *BALDASSARRE PERUZZI. Pittura, scena e architettura nel Cinquecento*, Rome 1987

– *RAFFAEL. Das architektonische Werk*, Stuttgart 1987.

– "LA VILLA Madama e la tipologia della villa romana nel Rinascimento", *Bollettino del Centro Internazionale di Studi di Architettura Andrea Palladio*, 11, 1969 (1970).

– "LA VILLA MÉDICIS et la typologie de la villa italienne à la Renaissance", *La Villa Médicis*, Rome 1991.

GAVALLOTTI CAVALLERO, D., *I palazzi di Roma dal XIV al XX secolo*, Rome 1989.

GERSTFELDT, O. von, *Römische Villen*, Leipzig 1909.

GOLZIO, V., *Palazzi Romani dalla rinascita al neoclassico*, Bologne 1971.

GREGOROVIUS, F., *Storia della città di Roma nel Medio Evo*, Rome 1900.

GROSS, H., *Roma nel Settecento*, Bari 1990.

HASKELL, F., *Mecenati e pittori. Studio sui rapporti tra arte e società italiana dell'età barocca*, Florence 1966.

HERMANIN, F., *La Farnesina*, Bergamo 1927.

HIBBARD, H., *Carlo Maderno and Roman Architecture*, London 1964.

IL CAMPIDOGLIO di Michelangelo, Milan 1965.

IL QUIRINALE, Rome 1974.

JANNONI SEBASTIANINI, C., *Le piazze di Roma*, Rome 1972.

LAIS, G., *Il terzo centenario della morte di San Filippo Neri a Palazzo Massimo*, Rome 1983.

LAUREATI, L. and TREZZANI, L., *Patrimonio artistico del Quirinale*, Rome 1993.

LEFEVRE, R., *Villa Madama*, Rome 1973.

LE PALAIS Farnese, Rome 1980-1981.

"LES FRESQUES NEOPOMPEIENNES du palais Taverne", *Connaissance des Arts*, 177, 1966

LIZZANI, M., *Palazzo del Quirinale*, Rome, no date.

LOMBARDI, F., *Roma, palazzi, palazzetti e case (1200-1870)*, Rome, 1991.

MANILLI, J., *Villa Borghese fuori Porta Pinciana*, Rome 1650.

MATTHIAE, G., *Roma Barocca*, Novara 1974.

MUNOZ, A. and COLINI, A.M., *Campidoglio*, Rome 1931.

NEPPI, L., *Palazzo Spada*, Rome 1975.

OLTRE RAFFAELLO, Rome 1984.

PALAZZO RONDININI, Rome 1983.

PALAZZO RUSPOLI, Rome 1992.

PECCHIAI, P., *Palazzo Taverna a Monte Giordano*, Rome 1963.

PERTICA, D., *Villa Borghese*, Rome 1990.

PORTOGHESI, P., *Roma Barocca*, Rome 1967.

– *ROMA nel Rinascimento*, Milan, no date

RENDINA, C., *I Papi: storie e segreti*, Rome 1983.

ROSATI, F., "Palazzo Altieri ieri e oggi", *Capitolium*, 49, 1974.

SALERNO, L., *Palazzo Rondinini*, Rome 1965.

SCHIAVO, A., *Michelangelo architetto*, Rome 1949.

– *PALAZZO della Cancelleria*, Rome 1964.

– "I PALAZZI dei Massimo", *Palazzo Braschi e il suo ambiente*, Rome 1967.

SPAGNESI, G.F., *Giovanni Antonio de Rossi*, Rome 1964.

TAFURI, M., *La via Giulia*, Rome 1973.

TIBERIA, V., *Giacomo Della Porta*, Rome 1974.

TOMEI, P., "Un elenco dei palazzi di Roma al tempo di Clemente VIII", *Palladio*, 1939.

– *L'ARCHITETTURA a Roma nel Quattrocento*, Rome 1942.

TONELLI, G., *Ville di Roma*, Rome 1968.

TOSELLI, G., *Palazzi di Roma*, Milan 1965

TORSELLI, G., *La Galleria Doria Pamphili*, Rome 1969.

VIA DEL CORSO, Rome 1961.

VILLA BORGHESE, Exhibition catalogue, Rome 1966.

VOSS, H., *Die Malerei des Barock in Rom*, Berlin 1924.

WITTKOWER, R., *Art and Architecture in Italy 1600-1750*, Harmondsworth 1975.

WURM, H., *Der Palazzo Massimo alle Colonne*, Berlin 1965.

ZACCAGNINI, C., *Le ville di Roma. Dagli "horti" dell'antica Roma alle ville ottocentesche*, Rome 1976.

ZERI, F. and MORTARI, L., *La Galleria Spada in Roma*, Rome 1970.